Great is Your Faithfulness

Memoir of David Rees

David Rees

Grosvenor House
Publishing Limited

This book is published by
Grosvenor House Publishing Ltd
Link House
140 The Broadway, Tolworth, Surrey, KT6 7HT.
www.grosvenorhousepublishing.co.uk

A CIP record for this book
is available from the British Library

ISBN 978-1-83975-215-5

To my sons, Paul, Stephen and Andrew and my wife, Jean without your encouragement this memoir would not have been written. To my dear grandchildren, Nathan, Zachary, Daisy, Amy, Bethany, Molly, Rosie, Tom, Winnie, Tilly, Betsy and Vivi, you have been the reason why this has been written; a record of your roots which I trust will give you a window to the past and provide inspiration for the future.

Table of Contents

Preface

This memoir was written during one of the most difficult periods for our generation. The coronavirus was on the march, the country in lockdown and death was dominating the news. Confined to our homes, I was encouraged by my family to use the time wisely and document my background and the stories that have shaped me personally and as a consequence my family. This is what I have sought to do in this document, somewhat imperfectly, so that the Rees clan; sons, daughters-in-law, grandchildren and any, great-grandchildren; can be given a window into the past to understand and interpret their heritage.

When I was writing this, I was asked to give a meditation for our prayer fellowship at Charlotte Chapel, Edinburgh. I include this meditation here, as part of my preface, as a reminder of the time we were living in. Also, to acknowledge that our lives are caught up in a sovereign, cosmic purpose where the victory and the glory belongs to God, and to God alone.

"Facing as we currently do unprecedented times, where life as we know it has had to be suspended and where the future appears uncertain and very much under threat, there is a dark foreboding and fear permeating the world. There is the fear of economic ruin, ill health and even a premature death. We have the surreal feel that the horsemen of the apocalypse have been unleashed across the world, as we see images of ghost cities that have been economically emasculated. There is the stench of death everywhere and we have resorted to the metaphor of war to describe our current plight, facing an enemy that is invisible, powerful, silent and devastating.

How does the Christian believer respond and react to this? Recently I have been reading the biography on 'Churchill – Walking with Destiny', by Andrew Roberts.

*It is 7 December 1941, when USA declared War on Japan. Churchill writes in his war memoirs of his euphoria that evening: 'Being saturated and satiated with emotion and sensation, I went to bed and **slept the sleep of the saved and thankful**' [2018, p693]*

The words that caught my attention are 'slept the sleep of the saved and thankful'. Churchill when he crafted those words, was thinking of final victory in WW2. However, in the context of our current challenges, the Christian believer, whose life is anchored to the Saviour of the world, can also speak of 'the sleep of the saved and thankful'.

The reason for this is that we have been redeemed by the blood of Christ. We know that: "Salvation belongs to our God, who sits on the throne, and to the Lamb" [Rev. 7:9] and we can shout our Hallelujah! because 'Salvation and glory and power belong to our God....' [Rev. 19:1].

When John was caught up to heaven [Rev. 4:1-3], he sees an opened door which is a door of revelation, which enabled him to have God's perspective of the future. What first confronted him is a throne, with one seated on the throne. This is a powerful reminder to us that God is King; the Lamb reigns and he rules over the Universe. So, whatever happens, however events unfold, we can all be secure in the knowledge that we are in the Lord's hands and he will bring us securely to his Kingdom. We have no assurance that we will escape the impact of the pandemic, nevertheless, we can sleep the sleep of the saved and thankful, because we know the ultimate victory belongs to God."

May it please God to bless this memoir to my family and anyone else who may read it, to the glory of His great and Holy Name.

David Rees
June, 2020

1

WHERE THE STORY BEGAN

Penygroes, which can be translated as 'top of the cross', is the village where I was born and where I spent the first 21 years of my life. It is a village in Carmarthenshire, and is located in the Mynydd Mawr [Big Mountain] area of the Gwendraeth Valley.

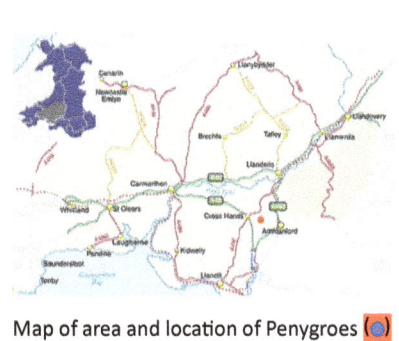

Map of area and location of Penygroes ⦿

To the North and North West, you have the Towy Valley with the picturesque and ancient towns of Llandeilo and Carmarthen. To the East you have the Black mountains, which is part of the Brecon National Park. To the South East the town of Ammanford and the Amman Valley and to the South and South West the towns of Swansea and Llanelli and the Swansea valley.

It is central to some beautiful landscapes, never far from mountains, valleys, the coast and towns. A local attraction that enriched one's appreciation of wild life when growing up was, Llyn Llech Owain, one of the finest beauty spots of Carmarthenshire with a variety of flora, fauna and wildlife.

Llyn Llech Owain

It is an area that was deeply affected by the Welsh revival of 1904. Indeed, the whole area quickly became known as *'the mountain of the blessing of God'*. Further details of this are given in Appendix I, which is the address I gave at the centenary service of Eglwys Efengyledd in Oct. 2010.

The area covering the Gwendraeth Valley is one of Wales' most Welsh of places. The valley is a stronghold of the Welsh language. Statistics show that it is the most Welsh speaking area in Carmarthenshire and one of the most Welsh speaking regions in all of Wales.

In terms of the evolution of the village, back in 1815 it consisted of a few thatched cottages and scattered farms[1]. What transformed the hamlet to a thriving village was the discovery of coal in the area. The development of the mining industry was accelerated when a Scotsman named Mr Ray moved into the district around 1840's to mine the coal seams.

Emlyn Colliery

This resulted in the sinking of a number of mines in the area, not least the Emlyn Colliery at Penygroes, which was opened in 1893 and closed in 1939. The pit produced the much sought-after anthracite coal. It was at this colliery that Lewis Rees, commenced his employment, working down the mine at the age of 14.

The village has a primary school. It also has a Rugby Union club, affiliated to the Welsh Rugby Union and a cricket team which plays in the Carmarthenshire League.

The village was well known as the headquarters of the Apostolic Church [see Appendix I for something of this history and its relationship to Eglwys Efengyledd]. The denomination hosted their International Convention in the village every year from 1916–2002. The church moved its main office to Swansea in 2002 but they still have their Bible college and substantial land in the locality.[2]

Eglwys Efengyledd, Penygroes   Apostolic Church, Penygroes

To get an insight into the insularity of village life let me tell you a story. A friend of mine, Prof. Colin Williams, who lectured at Cardiff University in the Celtic Studies Department was carrying out a survey across Wales on the implementation of the Welsh Language Act. He visited Penygroes, and one of the questions he would ask people was "had they any concerns?". At this particular house, back came the reply that they had real concerns and their concern was the number of foreigners moving into the area. My friend thought the foreigners were those who had crossed over Offa's Dyke. No, that was not their problem, their problem was the 'Swansea Jacks' that had moved into the area!

2

ROOTS - MY FATHER - LEWIS REES

Lewis was born in the year 1897, the son of John and Ann Rees from Ton-Ystrad, Rhondda, who married on the 13th August, 1887. My grandfather John was a colliery worker and he moved to Penygroes to work at the Emlyn Colliery. They had 7 children, four daughters Agnes, Margaret, Sarah, Beatrice, and three sons, Tom, Will and Lewis. [Appendix III gives the family tree of Lewis Rees.]

Lewis started work at 14 at Emlyn Colliery, although he had the opportunity to go to Grammar School, he decided against this. Whether this was his decision or his parents I don't know. He was an articulate man, a reader and a scribe. He also was an able violin player.

His first stint as a miner was interrupted by WW1 where he enlisted for active service with the South Wales Borders Regiment; although he was not old enough to enlist [he lied about his age]. The South Wales Borders regiment were engaged in active service at both Passchendaele and the Somme.

Lewis [Left] with brother Tom

5

He however was given an assignment to operate behind enemy lines in France, as part of a reconnaissance group. He was wounded in action when they were reconnoitring a farmhouse – specific details are somewhat hazy but he was apparently lost in action for four days, before being found. He was eventually discharged from the army but was promoted to Sergeant during this mission.

When he returned to civilian life he continued to work as a miner but this time at Cross Hands Colliery. He then moved on to work for Holwill, a haberdashery and oil company and took their mobile van around the farms of Carmarthenshire. The Company had an outpost in Carmarthen [the manager was Mr Welsh, a founding member of the Gospel Hall in Carmarthen]. The Company headquarters was in Swansea and owned by Chilcott, a committed Christian who attended Treboeth Gospel Hall. Chilcott bought the building which is now Ebenezer Gospel Hall in Blue Street, Carmarthen. Lewis finished his working life as a gardener and lorry driver for the National Coal board, working in Tumble. It was during this time that he became great friends of Winston Griffiths [Fforestfach], who also drove a lorry for the NCB. Winston is the father of Brian Griffiths, who headed Margaret Thatcher's kitchen cabinet, and now sits in the House of Lords as Lord Griffiths of Fforestfach.

In 1920 he married Mary Jane Evans, from Capel-y-Hendre.

Wedding Day outside the family home Aaron House, with my Grandfather, John. In the second row, Will, my mother's Brother with his wife Rachel Ann. [1920]

They had six children, the first two were sons, Hubert and Winston, but sadly they both died of pneumonia within the first year of life. They then had two sons, Peter [1925], John [1926], followed by a gap of 13 years, when Ann was born in 1941 and David was born in 1943

If I were to identify the most important event in the life of my parents, then I would unquestionably say that it was Lewis's conversion to Christ. Everything else about his life was shaped by this. Lewis was brought up in a non-conformist home and was taken regularly to the chapel and attended Sunday school. He would have been quite a young child when the 1904 revival broke out and so his personal awareness of the revival hardly registered with him. However, he would have imbibed something of the spiritual atmosphere of the period but it was not until his late twenties when God broke into his life. He was then a married man, a father of two sons, both of whom had died.

He decided, and the reason for this decision to me is unclear, to go down to Carmarthen, travelling in a charabanc, with a number of believers from Mission Cerrig, [alternative name by which the Evangelical Church was known] who were going there to hold an open-air witness to proclaim the gospel.

Towy river and bridge, Carmarthen

My brother's Peter memory of this was that he had gone down to play rugby and ended up after his conversion with Lewis throwing his rugby kit into the river Towy. That is a great story but I am not sure whether it is completely true.

The one fact that is certain is that he did attend the open-air service, which was held in Carmarthen Square, in front of what was then the Council building. It was here that the light of the gospel dawned on him, when he passed from darkness into light, and Lewis was never the same again.

The journey down in the charabanc was eventful in that it went off the road beyond Tumble. Lewis's take on this in later life was that behind that accident there was a sinister hand, the devil himself, who did his utmost to hinder Lewis Rees attend the open-air meeting. However, God's purpose could not be thwarted; there was no power on earth or in hell that could have changed the appointment that Lewis Rees had with the Lord, at Carmarthen square.

His destiny had already been determined; his name was in the Lamb's book of life, written there by divine decree from eternity past. So, what took place at Carmarthen Square, was his meeting with destiny, when God's mercy was poured into his life.

The Square, Carmarthen

My brother, John, who passed away August, 2015, recalled occasions when growing up, he would go down with Dad shopping in Carmarthen, and there was not an occasion when Lewis didn't go to Carmarthen Square and bow the knee to thank God for 'seeing the light' [John's words].

The reality of what took place in Carmarthen Square powerfully remained with him for the rest of his life, shaped his outlook and determined his priorities. We as children, (Ann, Peter, John and David), thank God for godly parents who taught us the gospel. In one of his books that I recently came across, are written the words: 'Saved by Grace' at Carmarthen Square, 18th February, 1922, Lewis Rees.

Ann Rees, Lewis Mum

Lewis was passionate for the gospel. He regularly preached at his own church, Eglwys Efengyledd and also in the surrounding mission halls. [Appendix II gives an insight into East Carmarthenshire's Mission Hall Saints.] He was part of the leadership of the church, although they did not have an official eldership or deaconate, they were very democratic in having a 'brethren' meeting', where decisions were made. This was not the best of models for church government, certainly didn't have a biblical mandate but it worked after a fashion!

My father in later life suffered badly from pneumoconiosis and emphysema, and this was what eventually took him. He was taken to Llanelli hospital having struggled for a number of weeks with his breathing and he passed away into the presence of his Lord, on January 2nd, 1967.

Cameos of Lewis Life

Cameo 1 - Proclaimer.

On a Sunday, we as family attended Church, both morning, afternoon (Sunday School) and evening. My Father in his earlier years as a Christian, would preach on the way to the Chapel. He would stop on his way up Waterloo Road, at strategic points and herald the gospel.

The church also would occasionally on a Sunday evening have an open-air service outside the Chapel, on the Square in Penygroes.

On one of these occasions, my second cousin, Wynne Davies, minister of St David's Church in Aberystwyth until his retirement in 2003, recounts this story[3].

Penygroes Chapel on the square

It was in response to the question about the chapels in the Penygroes of his youth, and specifically, was there an element of competition between these various churches and the chapels? This was his reply:

'Oh yes. My grandfather's brother, my Uncle Lewis, was a Plymouth Brethren, and attended the free evangelical Church. They would take part – as the Apostolic Church would, and the others – in open air meetings on a Sunday night. There they would be, at their various stands, preaching at the people who attended chapel. Indeed, when I first started preaching at the Welsh Calvanistic Methodist Church, my Uncle Lewis was preaching outside! He called to see my grandmother the following week, and I told him how surprised I was that he found it necessary to come and preach the gospel outside the church. And, of course, with his sense of humour – typically South Wales-he said, 'Well, it doesn't harm anybody to hear the gospel twice.'

On other occasions they would stand outside the Farmers Arms on the Penygroes square, and my Father when he saw people tumbling out of the pub, intoxicated with bottles in their hand, would proclaim the invitation of the gospel, that a well in the heart is better than a bottle in a pocket! The well giving living waters that only the Lord Jesus could give, from which we are fully satiated and thirst no more.

The story is told of Lewis calling out Scripture texts at one end of a street in Penygroes and being answered at the other end by the founder of the Apostolic church, Pastor Dan Williams. It would not be out of character for Lewis to respond back with the shout 'Bendigedig' [Praise Him].

Cameo 2 – Advocate and Counsellor

Idwal [left], Sarah, Lewis [4th from left], Alwyn Jones holding John.

One of Lewis Rees best friends and soul mate was Idwal Lewis of LLwynhendy. We were friendly with them as a family, Sarah, Idwal's wife was a good friend of my mother, Mary. Idwal was younger than Lewis and my father was very much his spiritual mentor. Both Idwal and Alwyn preached at my mother's funeral service.

Idwal was a conscientious objector in WW2 and had to appear before an appeal court in London, following an initial hearing in Carmarthen. My father acted on his behalf, speaking in his defence, which resulted in his appeal being successfully upheld. My father represented a number of people in this way and when he was in London, he took the opportunity to preach at Speakers corner in Hyde Park.

WW2 Gas Mask

When WW2 broke out and the Germans started bombing the UK, the government issued gas masks, which clearly was a very practical response to an imminent threat. This however to the pietistic world view of some devout Christians was not a straight forward issue.

The question was asked: *"Should we not trust in God"*. This was a real burden to Idwal, a question he agonised over, so he decided to consult the prophet Lewis Rees of Penygroes.

He came up by bus to see my Father [a distance of about 12 miles], and ask him the question: *"Lewis, have you had a word from the Lord, should we wear gas masks or not"*. Back came the reply from Lewis: *'No gas masks, Idwal'*. And so, it was no gas masks! We may smile at this or even have a degree of scepticism, but what this shows is that they had a faith that was real and however misguided, they wanted to honour the Lord.

One of our neighbours living four houses up from us was a Mr Edward Hughes. He was known as 'Hughes the Coop', because he worked in the Cooperative in Gorslas. Hughes, was a devout Christian, a hymn writer who contributed to the Hymnal, "Hymnau o Fawl" [Hymns of Praise], which we used in our Church in Penygroes. Hughes attended the Gospel Hall in Cross Hands and after one Sunday morning service he came, deeply distressed to see my father. It appeared that Mr Edward Wilkins, who had served as a missionary out in South Africa for a number of years from 1908, shared with them that morning an encounter he had had the previous day, with the Lord Jesus.

Mr Wilkins was out on a walk, and who drew near to him, walked with him and talked with him was Jesus. It was like an Emmaus road experience. The presence of Jesus was so real to him that when they came to a wicket gate, Mr Wilkins stopped and said to Jesus: "Cer Di gyntaf, Arglwydd" [You, go first, Lord]. I have no knowledge of the content of the conversation between the Lord and Wilkins, but one thing I do know, that Hughes was very distressed by what he heard, because he had never had an experience of the Lord like this. He was wondering whether there was anything spiritually out of tune in his life. I don't know what my Father said to Hughes the Coop, but he did leave somewhat more reassured and calmer.

Mr Wilkins was undoubtedly a godly man though eccentric. I remember him once sharing his anguish about whether he should bring the radio into the home. He resolved this dilemma by placing on the radio the words 'Holiness to the Lord' and of course he had Old Testament precedent for such a practice!

I will include one more story, that does not seamlessly fit into this section, but the link is Hughes the Coop. The group of churches that were known as Mission Halls, held a preaching service once a month, around the different halls. The format was 'Open Platform'. This meant that anyone who felt that they had a message from the Lord, would be free to share it, provided they were quick enough to get to the pulpit! On this occasion, we were in Bryn Seion, Cross Hands and Hughes was in the pulpit. He was deeply affected by the hope of heaven, and was warming to his subject, waxing eloquently in the climatic words, with his hands uplifted, that it would be "gogoniant I fe" [glory for me].

Irelian Jones with my father
[Oct., 1962 - Ann's 21st Birthday]

As he reached this high point, a voice came from the congregation: "Nage, Nage, dim gogoniant i fi, gogoniant iddo Fe" [No, No, it is not glory for me it is glory for Him].

It was Irelian Jones of Maesypont, quite a remarkable character who I will comment on in 'All things' Perkins chapter. This left Hughes somewhat perplexed, dumbfounded and deflated.

Cameo 3 – Seeking First God's Kingdom

Peter, the eldest son of Lewis and Mary was a gifted rugby player and was chosen to play for Wales in 1947, as a wing. I will come back to this again later.

Rugby was not seen as a neutral activity within the evangelical circle that my father moved in. He himself was a gifted rugby player, and played outside half for Penygroes Rugby Club. He was also an ex-captain of Penygroes but once converted he gave all that up. A major concern that he had was that Rugby could be elevated to an idol and lead people into worldliness and ungodliness.

Lewis in one of his preaching dialogues with the public made the statement that he would much prefer that Peter would have been a forward for Jesus Christ than play wing for Wales. Some Wag from the crowd shouted out: 'Off side, Lewis'! On another occasion, when he was heckled with the barbed comment, "You've got a slate off", Lewis responded, "That's when the Light shone in"!

My father's response to being congratulated by a village neighbour, Pugh Jones on Peter's international selection was: "It would have given me far greater joy if instead of a Welsh cap, Peter had received the crown of eternal life from Jesus Christ the Lord".

Cameo 4 – Grateful Praise

I have in my possession the words of a song that is titled: 'Collier's Saved Song'. I received it from my father, and I am uncertain who wrote it. It may well have been Lewis himself. Here are the words, to be sung to the tune of 'Be in Time'.

| 1. There's a word to me so dear
   In the pit with Jesus near
   I can read my title clear
   "Jesus Saves"
   For when darkness filled my soul
   And my sins were black as coal,
   By his stripes he made me whole "Jesus Saves." | 2. Grace there is to make me fit
   To shout "glory" in the pit
   When the lumps of coal I hit
   "Jesus Saves"
   Let the coal be soft or hard
   Working by the day or yard
   Perfect peace is my reward
   "Jesus Saves" |

Chorus: "Jesus Saves, Jesus Saves" From the fear of pit explosion "Jesus Saves" In the pit from sin set free Sudden death would "glory" be That is why I sing with glee, "Jesus Saves"	3. Mates have often at me laughed Often said that I was daft Singing in the coal pit shaft "Jesus Saves" But in spite of all their rubs And the deputy who snubs While I wait for empty tubs "Jesus Saves".
4. While descending in the cage For to earn a living wage I can sing while others rage "Jesus Saves" We black diamond for them get Though they force us hard to sweat There's salvation for them yet "Jesus Saves"	5. Set the joyful news abound On the top or underground That where ever man is found "Jesus Saves" Though the pit cap he lays down He will rise to wear a crown And go singing round the throne "Jesus Saves"

I go back to a holiday in Weymouth, with my father and my sister, Ann. Mum passed away the previous year. We were on holidays with family friends, Will and Maggie Davies. It was Sunday evening at the Christian hotel we were staying at. It was a fellowship evening where the custom was for guests to perform for the mutual enjoyment of the gathered company. Well, my father with his friend Will sang this song. This was to the profound embarrassment of Ann, myself and also Maggie's, who repeatedly poked her husband to get him to shut up! As far as Lewis was concerned, nothing would hinder or embarrass him from singing "Jesus Saves". He was an innate performer, supremely confident with an insatiable zest to relate to and entertain people.

3

ROOTS - MY MOTHER - MARY JANE REES, nee EVANS

Very little is known about Mary's parents. Mary was very reluctant to talk to any of her children about her parents. When Mary got married her mother had died and also her father.

Mary Jane Evans [My mother]

There were 5 children from the marriage, William, Idwal, Evelyn, Rachel and Mary Jane.

William got married to Rachel Ann and had one daughter Rhianedd. Idwal, remained a bachelor. Evelyn got married to Tom and had two children, Edna and Douglas. Rachel married Morgan Thomas and had two children, Glyn and Edmund.

Mary was born in 1901. When she married Lewis both attended Penygroes chapel, however neither appeared to have a saving faith. It was later in their marriage, when they experienced God's grace in salvation. Lewis conversion has already been detailed, and it appears that Mary's trusted soon afterwards.

My memories of Mum were of a loving, caring mother. She was first and foremost a Mum, a home-bird, who cherished everything relating to the family. As we have seen when considering Lewis, she had four surviving children, Peter, John, Ann and David. She had immense pleasure in ensuring that 'her children' were turned out the best.

Mary and Lewis, Rachel and Will [1921]

She was very hospitable. Invariably, the visiting preachers would either be staying at 93 Waterloo Rd [our home], or she would be having them for tea. Sunday was a busy day, and if the preacher was coming, then the tea table was always lavishly spread, covering all kinds of cakes and sweet dainties. Looking back at this now and knowing that she cooked everything in an oven heated by a coal fire, it was a herculean task.

David, Peter, Ann and John [2006]

Everything seemed to be so wonderfully cooked and presented; despite the vagaries of cooking in an oven whose temperature you couldn't regulate that well. However, my experience was of an even keeled mother, who was remarkably sweet tempered and took this heavy load of entertaining in her stride – she had a particular affection for me who she referred to as 'Dafydd bach' [literal translation 'little David' but it was used as a term of endearment]

She was wonderfully supportive of Lewis, particularly his work for the Lord and his activities at Eglwys Efengyledd. Church life was not always easy and I remember tensions that had arisen between the leaders in the fellowship, however Mum remained a great strength during those times of difficulty. She was a peace loving; gentle person and she took it very keenly if Lewis was the object of attack or criticism. As a young lad, I never understood the reasons for the underlying tensions, but I was sufficiently aware of them to recognise that there were certain tribal loyalties in the church, which polarised attitudes and caused a lot of grief.

Mary was exceptionally proud of her children's achievements. When Peter was selected to play rugby for Wales, it was an occasion of celebration for not only the family but also for the whole of Penygroes. However, Lewis, since his conversion to Christ, had put rugby behind him, and consequently he felt it was his duty, when the international match was on, that he was seen to be not listening to the match, and so he was working out in the garden. However, Mary had her ear to the radio, and gave regular updates to Lewis on the progress of the game!

Penygroes as we have already seen was primarily a mining community and working class. I remembering overhearing Mum, saying to a friend, after John had graduated and starting working with the National Coal Board that he was now on a 4-figure salary! This for an ordinary working-class family was a break-through achievement and Mary knew it and was justifiably proud of it.

Mum took immense pride in paying her bills on time. She was not going to have a red letter, indicating a late or missed payment from the South Wales Electricity Board, which the postman would see when delivering the post. Oh no, that was not going to happen to her! What would the neighbours think?

This kind of integrity is borne out by entries in the diary of Dafydd Perkins from Maesypont, a market gardener who used to sell produce to my mother. For example: Tuesday, June 4th, 1929 – 'Went to Penygroes with butter and eggs' - Among a list of names was the following: 3lbs of butter, 3doz eggs - Mrs Lewis Rees – paid 8/6 [8 shillings and six pence]. Every entry relating to my mother was paid. That was not true of a lot of other customers!

This diary came into my possession because I had the privilege of marrying his granddaughter, Jean Perkins in 1965.

Machpelah Cemetery, Penygroes

My mother passed away in 1958, at the relatively young age of 57. I will comment on the impact this had on my life, in the chapter that relates to me.

The funeral service took place at Capel Seion, an Independent Chapel because Eglwys Efengyledd would not have been in any way big enough for the large number of people who attended. The service was an amalgam of preaching, thanksgiving and memorial and it was long. It was a glorious celebration of the gospel of Christ, death's power had been broken through the death and resurrection of Jesus Christ.

There were two preachers, one gave a sermon in Welsh, Idwal Lewis, and the other in English, Alwyn Jones, who was a missionary out in the Caribbean but was home on furlough at the time.

I can still remember the text of the Welsh sermon, 'Yn ol Efengyl Gogoaniant y Bendigedig Dduw' ['The Gospel of the Glory of the Blessed God'] [1 Tim. 1:11]. It was a sermon par-excellence. It had an eloquence and power that gave words wings, like an eagle caught up in the mesmerising power of the sun [Son], soaring into the lofty heights of God's power and grace in the gospel. That is a powerful memory - it poured comfort into my grieving heart. My mother was interned at Machpelah Cemetery, Penygroes.

4

SIBLINGS - PETER, JOHN AND ANN

Peter

Peter is the eldest, surviving son of Lewis and Mary. He was born on the 8th February, 1925 and of all the children the one that was the sportiest. Because of this prowess, he is the best known of the Rees children. After primary school he progressed to study at Gwendraeth Grammar School. Peter would see the word 'study' as a gross misrepresentation, because in his words his primary interest was chasing a rugby ball and chasing the girls. On reflection he would moderate that by saying, the girls chased after him!

He sees his time at the Grammar School as intellectually wasted. He left at the age of 14 and commenced work with Raymond Price, doing the 'milk round'. After a year, because it offered better pay, he went to work for the National Coal Board [NCB] at Cross Hands Colliery. This opportunity opened up for him through my Father.

Initially, he worked with the blacksmith as a striker and then went to work underground. He did this for 9 years but during this time he realised that if he was going to progress his career then he had to invest in study. So, he commenced evening classes at Ammanford Technical College and then went on to Llanelli Technical College and Swansea College of Technology; completing his Higher National Certificate in both Mechanical and Electrical engineering.

During this period of part-time study, an opportunity opened for him to join a graduate training engineering scheme with the

British Electrical Supply Company, now known as the 'Central Electricity Generating Board [CEGB], at Llanelli Power Station, He then moved on to Tyr John Power Station, Swansea as a Junior Engineer and then, to Carmarthen Bay Power Station, Burry Port as a Control Engineer. He completed his employment with CEGB as Shift manager.

Peter in his Welsh Rugby Top [1947]

Peter's first love was rugby and he honed his rugby skills by playing in war-time charity matches at Stradey Park. He was introduced to this by Bert Peel, of Tumble, who was the mine first aider and very influential in the rugby fraternity. He is the grandfather of the Welsh scrum half, Dwayne Peel. Peter was selected to play for an 'invitation team' against a team from the RAF. This brought him to the attention of the Llanelli committee and resulted in him being invited to play for them. It is recorded that Peter was the top try-scorer in his first season [1945/46] with Llanelli, with 15 tries. He also achieved that accolade in the 1947/48 season with 13 tries. His comment on this was *'not bad considering I only received those number of passes!'*.

Peter was chosen to play for Wales against Ireland and France in 1947. The match against Ireland was played at Swansea's St. Helen's rugby ground, when international competition returned after the Second World War. They won that match. Peter was encouraged to go North and play Rugby League, and although he would have earned more money, he decided against that because he was thinking about his long-term future. He stopped playing rugby for the Scarlets around this time so that he could focus on his studies, although he still played for Penygroes.

After completing his studies, Peter joined the Llanelli RFC Committee and become Chairman in 1966, and later became President, Life Member, Shareholder and now Debenture Holder.

Peter and David
Last match at Parc y Stradey before
moving to Parc y Scarlets. Oct 2008

Parc y Scarlets Past Presidents
Board Feb., 2009
[Peter with brother,
David and nephew Paul]

1972 Stradey Parc – Llanelli v NZ

One of Peter's claim to fame is that he was the architect behind the famous win that Llanelli had against New Zealand in 1972, when they beat them 9 points to 3. The rationale behind that claim is that he was the one who had invited Carwyn James to become their coach. He recalls the journey he made with his family to Llandovery College where Carwyn was the coach.

He persuaded him to come to Llanelli and eighteen months later he was appointed as the British Lions Coach for their visit to NZ. That proved an inspired choice of coach because not only did the Scarlets beat NZ, the Lions also won the test series, and Carwyn became the first coach to achieve that accolade.

Peter married Nesta John on 2nd April, 1955, at St Mary Magdalene Church, St Clears. Nesta pursued a career in nursing and did her training at Hill House, Swansea Isolation Hospital. She then worked at Tumble Isolation Hospital. It was during this time that she met Peter.

Penygroes, was noted in the 50's for its Saturday evening dance held at the memorial hall, and many of the nurses in Llannon, came over for that. That is where Peter and Nesta first met, on the dance floor. That is where their eyes engaged, and a fire was lit that ignited a romance that lasted for over 61 years of married life. That was a real delight to observe.

Peter & Nesta, started their married life by renting a flat that overlooked St Helens in Swansea. I was particularly excited by that because there was a glorious view of the St Helens playing ground and the thought of watching rugby and cricket matches, without paying was something I found very inspiring.

After a few years, they moved to Pembrey, and Peter built the house that they have lived in for the rest of their married life. He has been active in the community, serving as a JP for twenty years; a founding member of the 'Cefn Sidan' rotary club and was awarded the 'Paul Harries Fellow' award some ten years ago.

Nesta become a mother in 1958 when Mark was born. She was a caring mother and loving grandmother. Mark married Susan, and they have two sons, Steffan and Ioan, who were born in 1994. She passed away in the Summer of 2015, after a long illness. Peter passed away on August 7th, 2020, just after I had completed this memoir.

John

John was born in 1926. He was academically gifted and had a gentle disposition – the nearest he came to any sporting prowess was playing tennis and in later life, golf.

Dad, with John, both holding a Bible

As a child growing up, he was a strong admirer of my Father. He went with him when Dad was preaching in other chapels and Mission Halls, and it was reported that often he used to say to Dad: "If no one else enjoyed you Dad, I did!"

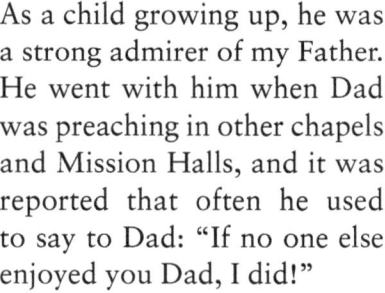

He passed his 11+ examination and went on to study at Amman Valley Grammar School in Ammanford.

From here he progressed to Cardiff University to study Mining Engineering, graduating with an Honours Degree in 1948.

John, graduating with Dad [1948]

One of his best friends, and the friendship continued throughout his life, was Albert Davies from Penygroes. Albert, did the same course as John and also came from a Christian family. His Father was known as 'Davies the Scribe' because he was the secretary of the Apostolic Church. They were a particularly gifted family. Albert went on to have a very successful career in the mining industry and with the Health and Safety Executive. He became at one point the President of his professional institution and on retirement became a Professor Emeritus in the School of Engineering at Cardiff University, giving lectures on health and safety in Industry. His brother, Gaius, was a medic and wrote a fascinating book on 'Stress, sources and solutions' published by Christian Focus in 1988. He also gave a tribute at the memorial service of Dr Martyn Lloyd Jones, looking at the Doctor from a medic's perspective.

My memory of that period was John and Albert entertaining us [me and my sister, Ann], with games played on the dining room table. We found that immensely entertaining. We really looked up to John and saw him as a person to emulate but at that stage in life I don't thing I understood the need for discipline and hard work, if one wanted to succeed.

John's first job after graduating was with the NCB, working in Cynheidre in the Gwendraeth Valley. The NCB were making bore holes in the area to locate coal mining seams and John's role was to assess the mineral deposits. He did this job for 2 years and then decided to pursue a career as a lecturer. His first post was at a College in Newcastle, and they bought a house in Whitley Bay, Tynemouth. Some years later, he was appointed as Head of Department of Mining at Wrexham College. He remained in this post until retirement. During this time, he became a Justice of the Peace.

John married Rhoda Williams from Cefneithin, on 14 Feb. 1953 who he met while working at the NCB. The Williams family were talented entertainers and her brother Ronnie became a double act on Welsh television, with Ryan Davies. It was known as 'Ryan & Ronnie', a television comedy series. They were the Welsh equivalent of the 'Morcombe and Wise' show.

John and Rhoda, had two children, Dylan [8 July, 1955] and Sian [27 June, 1961]. Dylan studied politics at Aberystwyth and after graduating pursued a career in the police force ending up as an Inspector. He pursued his political interest by becoming a Plaid Cymru candidate for Anglesey in the 2012 and 2017 general election, but on both occasions was not successful. He however remained active in local authority politics and became the Mayor of Anglesey. Sian did teacher training and became a teacher.

One story that is worth re-telling relates to Dylan's conversion experience. While serving in a Police station his Sergeant boss, witnessed to him and this resulted in Dylan becoming a Christian. When he was home with his parents, he asked his Mum, for Uncle David's telephone number. Rhoda's response to this was, "Don't ring up Uncle David, he will only try and save you!". Back came Dylan's response, "Mum, I have already been saved". At that point Rhoda called out: "John, John, get me a sherry, Dylan has been saved". God works in mysterious ways his wonders to perform!

John passed away in 2010, having been diagnosed with the human form of CJD and Rhoda predeceased him by three years.

Priscilla Ann

Ann was born on the 20th Oct, 1941. The long-sought for daughter had arrived. In Lewis' words, he and Mary had prayed for a daughter and the Lord very graciously, heard their prayers.

In what would have been viewed as Mum's middle age, she conceived and gave birth to a beautiful daughter. I can well imagine the joy and celebration that this visitation brought.

As events unfolded it was evidently the Lord's provision for Dad and myself, for in 1958 our mother passed away with terminal kidney cancer and Ann stepped in to care for us, and what a wonderful job she did.

Mary with her daughter, Ann [1942]

Ann, was gifted, particularly in music. She passed her examinations to enter Amman Valley Grammar school, just as her brother John had done. She was making good progress at the school and then came the seismic event, in her 'O' Level year, when Mum passed away. The decision was made, for better or for worst, for Ann to give up her schooling and look after the home, and take care of Dad and me. I look back with great gratitude for the love and care she showed her younger brother, and the way she sacrificially served.

I reflect on that now, still wondering how on earth that could have happened, because Ann had all the capabilities of progressing to University and becoming a teacher.

Ann and David on holiday, 1951

She continued with her Piano theory and practical examinations and achieved Level 8 grade. She also, because of this had the opportunity to study at the Royal Academy in London, but circumstances made it impractical for her to take this offer up. She put her musical gifts to good use by teaching privately at home, but it goes without saying that this did not in any way compensate her for giving up the opportunity of a good career outside the home.

Ann become a Christian in her teens. I remember an occasion when she shared her testimony at the Mission in Lamas Street, in Carmarthen. She was articulate and what we in Wales would say 'ar tan' ['on-fire']. It was a wonderful testimony to the saving grace of God. Why the Mission and not the gospel hall in Blue Street? Well, the mission hall allowed women to speak but this was forbidden in Blue Street. I recall that I also gave my testimony that evening, but I found the experience very intimidating and I had hardly started before I froze and so I had to come down. That didn't happen with Ann!

Ann got married to Graham Lord of Caerphilly in Eglwys Efengyledd, Penygroes, on 14th March, 1966. They had one off-spring, Helen who went on to do a teacher training degree at Trinity College, Carmarthen. Helen is also gifted musically. She is the mother of triplets, Sion, Stephen and Dafydd and is married to Robert Mills.

14th March, 1966. Wedding of Ann and Graham Lord at Eglwys
Efengyledd
Left to right: Peter, Nesta, John, Dylan, Rhoda, Mark, Graham, Ann,
Sian, Lewis, Jean, David

The Siblings together.

2003 - John & Rhoda' Golden Wedding Anniversary at the Stiwt
Theatre, Rhosllannerchrugog, Wrexham.
[Ann & Graham, Nesta & Peter, Rhoda & John, Jean & David]

5

'BONUS SON' – DAVID

I was born on the 28th April, 1943, the youngest child of Lewis and Mary. Some 20 months earlier my sister Ann was born. We were seen as the 'second hatch', with our mother giving birth to two babies in her early and mid-forties.

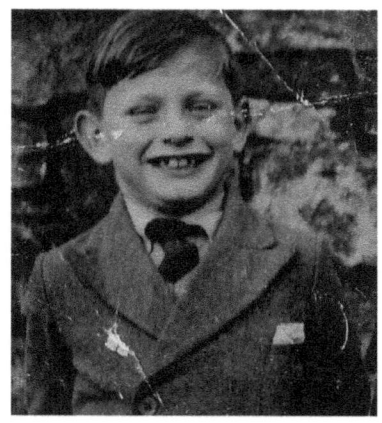

The significance of my birth can best be put in context by a wonderful quote from my father. I heard it when he was visiting the farms of Carmarthen in his Holwill van when I went occasionally with him during my summer holidays. He would introduce me in these terms: *"I prayed for a daughter and the Lord gave me, Ann; then David arrived as a 100% bonus"*. So, I was the surprise "bonus" son, it is for others to judge how well I have lived up to this auspicious description.

The local GP had a different take on the growth of the Rees family. He said to my Father: "Too much 'Life Drops' Lewis!". Lewis was a keen 'Life Drops' man, which he regularly took with his tea.

My recollections of childhood are of genuine happiness. We lived in 93 Waterloo Road, a semi-detached house, which had three bedrooms and two living rooms, one had rather the posh name of 'parlour', and was reserved for use on special occasions, like when we had visitors. We lived in the main in the 'living room', where we had the coal fire and oven. Off this room, was the 'room under the stairs', which we had a lot of fun with when growing up. I have recollections of hiding here, when we were entertaining the threat that the Germans were coming to bomb us! What I am not sure about, whether this was a game that we played, or it was actually during WW2, because if that was the case then I would have been very young. What I do know is that a bomb was dropped in the area, when the Germans were doing their bombing raids on Swansea.

93 Waterloo Road

There was also the larder, which was attached to the house and was very cold, an ideal place to store food and this was the place where Mum prepared our meals. During our early teens, an extension was built which provided us with a more formal kitchen and a bathroom. Prior to this, we used to bath in a tub by the fire and our toilet was outside at the bottom of the garden. My memory of growing up in those early years was to see my father and brothers having a tub bath, after returning from work. All three of them worked in a colliery at one period of their lives.

Since there was no central heating, the bedrooms were very cold during winter time. We got ready for bed during this time of the year, by changing in front of the fire and then rushing up as quickly as we could to snuggle into bed. I have great memories of enjoying reading, with my torch and being absorbed and sometimes frightened by reading 'The famous five' series of books by Enid Blyton, or the 'Biggles' series of books by Captain W. E. Johns.

Invariable the day finished with reading the Bible and prayer. My father used Scripture Union notes, and occasionally he would read to us extracts from John Bunyan, Pilgrim's Progress.

Since I was a child of the war years, economically life was tough for my parents, however, it was never something I was that deeply aware of. My father was a keen gardener – he had his own garden as well as a substantial plot in Aaron House, the home of his parents. So, in the main we lived off our own garden produce. He also had some chickens and on one occasion a pig – all kept at the top of the garden in a sty. To this day I remember the occasion when the local butcher came to kill the pig with the shrill scream of the pig being butchered.

By this time my father was suffering from pneumoconiosis and so breathing was a challenge for him, so I was asked to do a lot of the hard digging. It was never that stimulating and it always seemed to clash with other priorities like playing sports with my friends. I did my duty, but often it would be hurried so that I could escape as quickly as possible, to do what I liked doing.

I loved sport, all kinds of sport; rugby, cricket, tennis, running, snooker. I loved the outdoor life, cycling, exploring, hiding, swimming. In part this was a family trait but also shaped by having an older brother who was a talented rugby player and a Welsh international, which I have already written about. He was my role model. I have often said, that growing up I felt very important. I had a father who was very well known in the village, highly respected, articulate and an able lay preacher. I had a brother who was idolised because he had been chosen to play for Wales in Rugby. I believe he is the first person from Penygroes chosen to play for his country. In a rugby village, that was a great honour! Here was 'young Dafydd' who lived out his life in this reflected glory – yes, I did feel very important. My wife Jean, tongue in cheek will often say that, the sense of importance has not left me!

You will notice from what I have said so far, there are a couple of things missing. The first is football and the second is study. Let me now deal with these two in turn.

Penygroes School, Waterloo Road

I attended the primary school in the village and one of the 'sport masters', if they were called that then, was Mr John Evans. He loved rugby but despised the game of football. If anyone played in the School yard the round ball, he would confiscate the ball and make the barbed comment, *"Bachgen, byth rhaid i ti wisgo pais arnat ti"*. [*'You boys, you need to put a petticoat on'*]

So, from a young age there was antipathy towards football, because no boy would want to play a girl's game, would they?

As an aside, he was never a great teacher. He was a very staunch Labour supporter and on one occasion sought to win a parliamentary seat for Labour. He married late in life, Miss Bevan, who taught the scholarship class at the school. She was exceptionally good and prepared children well for their scholarship exams. He on the other hand was very lazy and invariably spent a lot of his time teaching poetry and from my recollection always stared at his figure nails! One poem stuck, William Wordsworth's:

'I wandered lonely as a cloud, That floats on high o'er vales and hills, When all at once I saw a crowd, A host, of golden

daffodils; Beside the lake, beneath the trees, Fluttering and dancing in the breeze.'

I have no recollection that I was a studious child growing up. Did I do homework? I must have done but I have no recollection of doing it. At the age of 11 one sat the scholarship exam to enter grammar school. All my siblings had jumped this hurdle without a problem, Peter went to Gwendraeth Grammar School and John and Ann went to Ammanford Grammar school. The expectation was that I would do the same. I will never forget the day when I learned that I had failed. I was walking up Waterloo Rd and coming towards me was my Headmaster, Mr Llewellyn. He pulled me aside and told me the bad news that I had failed the exam, and that I would now be progressing to Llandybie Secondary Modern School. That was quite a blow to me and in part may well have in a providential way shaped my future path, and produced a certain steeliness that eventually issued in a successful career.

I was given the opportunity two years later, through examinations to enter the Technical School at Ammanford. This school prepared students for the 'Ordinary National Certificate' in Technical studies, and was the foundation to pursue a career in engineering. It provided a feeder stream into continued studies at Ammanford Technical College.

Cameos of Childhood - Summer Holidays

The majority of the summer holidays for my contemporaries was spent in entertaining ourselves, by playing, cycling etc. The majority of us came from ordinary working-class homes and so the concept of going away on holidays was fairly foreign. We would very occasionally go on a day visit to Swansea Bay.

I do recall one holiday when I went with my Father to Llandrindodd Wells, to a Keswick in Wales conference. My mother stayed at home. The holiday could not have been that memorable as I have no recollection of it, apart from recalling my Father's interest in the spa facilities of the town and the content of the preaching!

Sunday School Trip [David & Ann [front-far right; Will Davies-top right]

What was very much anticipated was the Sunday School trip to the seaside, where we would go to different seaside resorts each year. I have memories of going to Saundersfoot, Tenby, Newquay and Llanstephen. Those are wonderful memories.

Dryslwyn Castle and Towy River

One of the enjoyments of the summer holidays, was cycling with friends to Dryslwyn Castle, and swim in the river Towy. We would take a packed lunch, prepared by our mothers, cycle through Maes-y-Bont, pass 'Golden Grove', a famous estate which is now an agricultural college, and go down and along the Towy valley, until we reached Dryslwyn Castle.

Beneath the castle, we dammed the river to give us a pool area that we could swim in. This was idyllic, refreshing after a long cycle, with glorious views of the countryside. Within our eye line would be the ancient town of Llandeillo and Dinefwr Castle, which also was perched along the river Towy.

Another cycle ride would have been to Carreg Cennen Castle in Trapp. This was idyllic countryside, with castle ruins to explore and plenty of places to play.

This represented a world very different from today, because growing up we were totally uninhibited about exploring the countryside without parental supervision and being away from home for many hours. Today's world seems so very different and it is not to do with age either!

One event that brought the people of Waterloo Road together was the coronation of Queen Elizabeth II on June 2nd, 1953. We had a celebration that culminated in a tea party and that was an event that really resonates in my memory.

Coronation Tea Party – Ann, [5th], David [11th], Wyn Davies [12th - 2nd cousin, quoted in Lewis section], John P Thomas* [13]

*Secretary of Eglwys Efengyledd at the time of its centenary [2010]. Passed away on August, 29th, 2018

Cameos of Childhood - Apostolic Convention

The August weekend holiday and the week that followed it was the week of the convention. Penygroes during this week was transformed into a hive of activity and was internationalised, with visitors coming from across the world. The school was converted to dormitories where visitors could stay. This for us was fun time! We used to sneak into the school, the week before visitors arrived and had pillow fights which was wonderfully invigorating, until we were found out and chased out of the school. This would not deter us; we always found a way back into the school!

Convention time was always an opportunity to make money. We built our carts and took them up to the square in Penygroes to meet people coming off the bus. Invariably, they came heavy laden with cases and so we would offer our services: '*Can we carry your bag please?*" and the offer was gratefully received and was profitable. However, there were exceptions. A friend of mine took these cases down to the extreme end of Gorsddu Road, which would have been about a mile and a half from the square and when they arrived at this particular house, he was thanked and blessed with the words: "*The Lord bless you my boy*", but there was no offer of payment. Back came the reply, pretty quickly: "*The Lord will carry your bags next time too!*"

I have memories of attending the late-night service at the convention, which often took the form of a testimony evening. We went not because of any deep spiritual interest but rather to be entertained. There were some extrovert characters, one lady from Penygroes comes to mind, who always seem to be restored to the Lord at convention time. During the rest of the year she seemed to live a very undisciplined life. When she joined the congregation, she always danced down the aisle waving a rather large handkerchief. It was a spectacular entry, to be observed and admired but to what extent it was a celebration of the joy of the Lord, I leave others to judge.

Cameos of Childhood - Emlyn Colliery: Ghosts of the night

Emlyn Colliery was now closed, but it had its coal tip and buildings, some of which were now in a state of disrepair. There was one building adjacent to Corsddu Road, which we had gained access to and we put to good use on dark evenings. We would dress up in sacks and fit hoods around our heads. We then would immerge out of the darkness, in our disguise and seek to frighten passers-by. I am not sure how successful that was. I always felt that we were more frightened than those we were trying to frighten. Be that as it may, it was great fun.

Another memory associated with Emlyn Colliery, was the occasion after I broke my leg in school. There was another friend,

Brian Edwards, in a similar position who also had broken his leg as the result of falling off a horse while racing. There was some rivalry between us, he was always viewed as something of a wild character, and I guess I was not far behind. We challenged each other to a cart race. Here we were, both with one leg in plaster facing up to what was no ordinary race. It had to be down one of the slopes of the coal tip. I cannot remember who won, but I do remember, and it was something that I was very worried about, that when I had to go back to Llanelli Hospital to have my plaster off, it was as black as the ace of spades.

Cameos of Childhood - Bringing in the Hay

Our home was located between two farms, Pant-y-blodau, and Brynclo. There was only one house between us and Pant-y-blodau and my father had a good relationship with the farmer. They were members of the Apostolic Church. I always looked forward to Summer-time particularly when the hay was brought in. It was very much a community endeavour, where neighbours helped local farmers. Hay was raked into piles, while others would pitch the hay on to the cart. I recall doing some work but my exhilarating memories are playing in the hay-stack, riding on top of the hay wagon with my sister Ann, and most important of all, the meal that we had after a day's hard work. It was the most wonderful of feasts, with delicious ham and all the supporting cast of salads and side dishes. Not least was the 'home-made' ginger beer which really slaked our thirst.

6

CHANGE OF HORIZON - SPIRITUAL ENCOUNTER

None of us are an island, we are shaped by so many different influences and as I reflect on my own life, I recognise the rich diversity of factors that has made me what I am today. The language of the home was Welsh and two dominant influences that impacted my upbringing are crystallised in two Welsh Songs:

Song 1: Sospan-fach: A traditional welsh folk song that catalogues the troubles of a harassed housewife – this song has been adopted by Llanelli Rugby Club, the Scarlets as their club anthem. The Scarlets official magazine is titled 'Sospan'.

Stradey Parc – Llanelli

Mae bys Meri-Ann wedi brifo,
A Dafydd y gwas ddim yn iach.
Mae'r baban yn y crud yn crio,
A'r gath wedi sgrapo Joni bach.
Sosban fach yn berwi ar y tân,
Sosban fawr yn berwi ar y llawr,

Dai bach y sowldiwr,
Dai bach y sowldiwr,
Dai bach y sowldiwr,
A gwt ei grys e mas.

The song speaks of Mary's finger being burnt, the baby crying, Joni being scratched by the cat, the saucepans on the fire boiling and Dai with his shirt hanging out of the back of his trousers.

Song 2: 'Dyma Cariad fel y Moroedd' [Here is love, vast as the ocean]: This hymn became very much the signature song of the revival, written by William Rees.

Verse1 – Welsh	Verse1 – English
Dyma gariad fel y moroedd, Tosturiaethau fel y lli: Twysog Bywyd pur yn marw - Marw i brynu'n bywyd ni. Pwy all beidio â chofio amdano? Pwy all beidio â thraethu'i glod? Dyma gariad nad â'n angof Tra fo nefoedd wen yn bod.	'Here is love, vast as the ocean, loving kindness as the flood, when the Prince of life, our ransom, shed for us his precious blood. Who his love will not remember? Who can cease to sing his praise? He can never be forgotten throughout heaven's eternal days.

Moriah Chapel, Loughor.

Moriah chapel became the centre of the 1904 revival.[4] It was the home church of Evan Roberts and it is to this church he returned to from West Wales to conduct a week's meetings. This proved significant in that many lives were transformed by the gospel and the work of spiritual renewal spread from Loughor to the surrounding areas.

So here we have two songs, representing two contrasting worlds, one the world of rugby and the other of evangelical Christianity. There is a sense in which our home was a microcosm of that contrast, as we have already seen, my eldest brother, Peter played rugby for the Scarlets and also played for Wales in 1947 and my father was a lay preacher and an elder at 'Eglwys Efengyledd', Penygroes. I cannot overemphasise how intoxicating a mix that was to a young lad like me, with a brother 19 years his senior who had played for Wales, and a father, well known in the village as a lay preacher.

These two worlds did not sit comfortably alongside each other within a pietistic evangelical tradition and I knew something of that tension growing up, loving rugby and all kinds of sport and having to face up to the challenge of the Gospel, of following Christ as Lord and Saviour.

Home was a caring and godly place where the name of Christ was loved and honoured. I was brought up to attend Church and hear God's word. Clearly, these were the two major influences that shaped my Christian mindset.

One individual, in particular I will mention, is Cyril Cann, who taught us in Sunday School. He came from Llanelli and married Meryl Thomas, whose family were members of Eglwys Efengyledd.

Cyril and Meryl Cann [1953] Cann.

Pendine Sunday School Trip with Cyril David – third from the right. [1954]

He was a mature student at Trinity College, Carmarthen, and during this period, while living with his in-laws, made Eglwys Efengyledd his spiritual home. He took us under his wings and organising outings for us on occasional Saturdays, when we would visit the seaside, places like Pendine. He would squeeze us all into his Ford Popular car, all 7 of us, and off we would go. That was a real treat.

I was impressed as a young boy with his well-ordered mind. Even now I can remember the first sermon I heard him give, it was on John 3, the encounter that Nicodemus had with Jesus and what lives in my memory was his ability to describe a scene and articulate a narrative. I can even today from his description, hear the patter of Jesus walking down the cobbled streets of Judea. I give God thanks for these spiritual inputs into my life. Cyril went on to pursue a career in education, and spent the latter years of his working life as a lecturer in the education department of Bristol University.

If you had asked me when I was a child what I believed, then I would have said that I uncritically accepted Christianity as true. I had great respect for my parents and real admiration for my Dad and there never crossed my mind the possibility that they could in any way be wrong. At what stage did the faith of my parents become mine? Or to put it within a more theological framework, when was I 'born-again' by God's Spirit?

There was a first experience, which led to a premature birth. I was around 10 years of age at the time and I attended the Sunday evening service. The preacher was a young man from Swansea Bible College. He was eager, passionate and clearly wanted to have a 'trophy' to take back to College. He confronted me after the service and asked whether I loved the Lord Jesus. My answer was, of course, I loved the Lord Jesus, what else could I have said. Well, that led the young man to say that I had been saved.

When I arrived home that Sunday evening, the news was announced to the family, with my two elder brothers present, that David had been saved! My brother's immediate response was, *"Well David, there is no more rugby for you then"*. I felt that taunt, like as if a sword had pierced my heart. Rugby was my first love. This was Sunday, and as the week progressed, I had an increased longing to see Penygroes play on Saturday, but I knew that if I went, then my brothers would see me and they would question my 'salvation experience'. I manage to resolve this dilemma by watching the match through the hedge of an adjacent field, which I had to reach by taking a detour through a number of fields, so that my brothers couldn't see me!

My authentic spiritual birth, took place some four years later, on November 9th, 1958. A number of factors led up to this, not least the passing away of my mother with liver cancer, earlier that year. That was a numbing experience which challenged so much of the security that had surrounded my life. I knew Mum had gone to heaven but I was not sure that I was going there as well. That was a worry to me.

As months went by the loss of mother was felt more acutely, and as the result of that started kicking over the traces. I was attracted to playing snooker, and I spent as much time as I could in the snooker hall, to the consternation of my father. I think he saw the danger of a misspent youth. The man in charge of the snooker hall, had a reputation of being an unsavoury character, and this accentuated my father's concern.

I also had started going out on a Saturday evening to Ammanford with some friends. There the young people gathered in their droves. It was the beginning of the teddy boy generation, some carrying lethal weapons like knuckle dusters. It was an opportunity for confrontation, menace and trouble, which had a strange form of attraction in that it appealed to my search for high drama. It was at this time that I saw my first cinema film. It featured Sophia Loren as the lead actress. It was not an experience that I was wholly comfortable with coming from a strict nonconformist family. The question was being raised, if not articulated in words, certainly it was one that was thought: "*Was David going down the slippery slope?*". I remember my brothers warning me that unless I pulled up my socks, I would end up down the coal mine, digging for coal for the rest of my life.

Things came to a head on the Sunday evening of November 9th, when the preacher at 'Mission Gerrig' was a young man from the 'Open Air Mission'. This was part of a week of evangelistic meetings, and was the final meeting. After he had preached, he gave a public invitation for people to stand if they wanted to indicate that they had accepted Christ as Lord and Saviour. I cannot remember what he preached on but what I do remember is the overwhelming conviction that God had spoken into my life and was calling me to faith and repentance. I responded to the invitation, stood-up and in tears bowed before the cross of Christ, recognising that he had borne my sins in his own body on the tree. That was my authentic new birth, when the faith of my parents became mine. I was made a new creation in Christ, and I knew it. That was the turning point in my life, and all the fears and tensions that were associated with my 'premature birth' disappeared. This was for real; it was my Damascus Road experience and everything from this point onward has shaped the course and direction of my life. My decisions, choices, priorities, hopes, aspirations, goals can all be traced to my encounter with the living Christ that Sunday evening. I would dare to claim that you will never understand me without looking through the prism of my new birth. For the sake of this record, I was baptised on the 28th June, 1960 in my home church.

One immediate outcome of becoming a Christian, was the putting right of previous wrongs. About a year earlier, I had my bike repaired at the 'cycle shop' in Norton Road, and at that time I didn't have any money on me for the repairs. I never told my parents this, but I conveniently forgot about this payment. After my conversion, I had a reawakened conscious, and so I was prompted to pay the cycle shop a visit to clear my debt of around two shillings and six pence.

It was the culture of the church to have open-air meetings for the proclamation of the Gospel. On Friday evenings the young people met at the memorial hall to dance. It was the beginning of the swinging sixties, where 'Rock and Roll' and the Teddy-Boy look were the fashion of the day. In fact, Penygroes had become the place to be for this kind of music. We held a gospel witness outside this location and I carried a banner with the words

'Prepare to meet thy God'. On one occasion I received the challenge: *"You are not brave enough to bring it inside the hall"*, and I instantly responded to the invitation. On taking it inside I was un-ceremoniously chucked out by the organisers, with the words ringing in my ear: "Get him out"!

7

OPPORTUNITIES BECKON - FIRST JOB AND EARLY STUDIES

Having successfully completed my Welsh Joint Education, S1 [Stage 1] in Engineering with two distinctions, one in Mathematics and the other in Engineering Science, I started work on 7th September, 1959, as an electrical apprentice with 'The Steel Company of Wales [SCOW]' based at Trostre Works, Llanelli, which was part of the Tinplate Division. .

This was a wonderful opportunity, which provided the platform for me to pursue a successful career in Electrical Engineering. This was the catalyst that fired my interest in 'Control Engineering', which became my main discipline as I pursued an academic career in later life, but more about that later. This opportunity came through my brother Peter and his rugby contacts. Apprenticeships were very sought after and I have no doubt that without Peter, then this door would not have opened for me. The apprenticeship was for five years and I was inducted in the installation and maintenance of rotating electrical plant, switchgear, control gear, including electronics and instrumentation, transformers, rectifiers and cranes. My five years was spent as follows: Apprentice School [12 months], Electrical Plant Maintenance [24 months], Electronics Department [6 months], Instrument Department [6 months], Drawing Office [3 months], Engineers' Office [3months], General Services [6 months].

I attended three Colleges during my apprenticeship, all on a part-time basis, day release and evening study during which I studied for my Higher National Certificate [HNC] and

Endorsements. These were Ammanford Technical College, Llanelli College and Swansea College of Technology and I was awarded my HNC in 1963, with three distinctions in 1963 and the following year I completed an endorsement subject in Electronics, which I passed with a distinction.

Receiving 'The South Wales Institute of Engineers' Scholarship Prize [1963]

As the result of these successes I was awarded 'The South Wales Institute of Engineers Scholarship grant' of £25 in October, 1963. I had previously won in 1960, an apprentice prize of £5 in the electrical group of apprentices at Trostre Works and then had 'The Institution of Electrical Engineers, Institution' prize in 1963, where I was awarded a cheque, the value of which I cannot remember, and a 'Certificate of Merit'. Only 30, out of 3000 students, who passed the HNC examination were awarded a prize of this nature. I document this to highlight that even 'no-hoper's' can succeed, and through God's gracious providence my inauspicious start was becoming a distant memory.

On completing my apprenticeship and receiving my internship, I decided that I would continue my studies by completing a degree course in Electrical and Electronic Engineering. I successfully applied to Swansea University for a place and I also won a three-year scholarship from SCOW to finance my studies and provide a comfortable living grant. This also provided me with employment at the Steel works during the Summer vacation.

'The Dragon', the monthly publication of the Steel Company of Wales in its November, 1964 edition, reported on my success in the following terms: "A Trostre electrical engineering apprentice who nearly topped a country wide results table when he passed his Higher National Certificate, has been granted a scholarship by our Company to enable him to study for a degree in Electrical and Electronic Engineering".

This meant that I studied at Swansea University, in the School of Electrical and Electronic Engineering, from Sept. 1964 to June 1967, graduating with a 1st Class Honours degree.

Graduating Ceremony [1968 – actually graduated in 1967]

This gained the attention of the 'South Wales Evening Post' a year later, on July 17th, 1968, with the headline: 'Degree after 11 plus failure'. It included this photograph of my graduation. I was not able to attend the ceremony in the summer of 1967, hence the one-year delay.

Studying at Swansea was intellectually an enriching experience and that proved very rewarding. In my final year project, I was allocated to a post-graduate research student, Jack Golten, who was working on the modelling of steel under-going reduction. We developed a 'Hybrid Computing' model of the steel rolling process and this resulted in my first paper which I jointly published with Jack Golten.[5] The equations that model the behaviour of steel undergoing reduction are complex differential equations, and the combination of analogue and digital techniques were necessary to solve them, in real-time. At least, that was cutting edge technology in 1966! This collaborative venture was my introduction to publishing in Scientific Journals and Conferences that continued throughout my career until I retired in 2010. I will return to this later in my memoirs.

What about my spiritual development? The period of the sixties was a time when there was a resurgence in reformed theology. Two key persons in that resurgence, was the Welsh preacher Dr Martin Lloyd Jones[6], Minister of Westminster Chapel, London and a young academic, Dr J I Packer[7], who had completed his PhD on one of the Puritans. IVP published his book 'Evangelism and the Sovereignty of God'[8] in 1961, which proved very influential in shaping a young generation of Christians. Around, the same time, aided and encouraged by these men, the publishing house 'Banner of Truth' was set up to revive interest in reformed and Puritan theology. In terms of the circle that my father moved in, these emphasizes would not have been foreign to me.

For example, Irelian Jones, a friend of my father would read John Owen's work on 'The death of death in the death of Christ'[9] and would have viewed it as his 'bread and butter' diet. What a diet!

Also, Lewis, Idwal and Irelian were known as 'bois y tick' [tick boys], because when a person was converted, they would speak of a tick being inserted against that person's name in the Lamb's book of life, because it had been written there from eternity past by divine decree.

I was very much influenced and stimulated by these developments and it helped to formulate my theological perspectives. This has been a great blessing to me through the course of my Christian life and has very much influenced my input into the life of my family. There is nothing more liberating than to know that salvation is a work of God and that *"He works out everything in conformity with the purpose of his will, in order..... our hope in Christ, might be for the praise of his glory"* [Eph. 1:11-12].

Many of my Christian friends, working at SCOW were similarly influenced. That is part of the story that is tinged with considerable sadness. One of my acquaintances, who had a lively interest in Calvin's Institutes and the works of John Owen, committed suicide. The primary reason for this was, that he was abused as a child and in adulthood he struggled with it to the point that he could not manage the pain any more. An adjunct to this pain was being disciplined by his local church for his Calvinistic views and it is unclear to me what contributed the most to his despair. After we had left Swansea, another friend ended up with a failed marriage. His wife was unfaithful to him by going off with his Christian friend, who she eventually married. Sadly, in the end both of them denied the faith and I have no knowledge whether they returned in repentance to the Lord. It is best to draw a veil over this part of my memory.

There were however very happy memories of fellowship in the gospel with a number of individuals. There was Peter Phillips, who left SCOW to pursue a career in banking and who later served as an elder and Bible teacher in Trimsaran Gospel Hall. Then Eddy John, a well-known and greatly respected Christian leader and preacher from Morfa, Llanelli who had a great heart for people and deeply burdened about their lostness without Christ. Finally, Eddy Edwards, who had a radical conversion experience in his early thirties, who also left SCOW and went on to study theology and serve as a Baptist minister in Swansea.

8

MATTERS OF THE HEART

I am coming to this part of my memoir, having just completed a Bible study using Zoom, with a group of men from the Men's Fellowship of Charlotte Chapel. The study was on Proverbs 30, and we reflected on the words: '*There are three things that are too amazing for me, four that I do not understand, the way of an eagle in the sky, the way of a snake on a rock, the way of a ship on the high seas, and the way of a man with a young women.*' [Proverbs 30:18-19]. The final item of '*the way of a man with a young woman*', is the true wonder of the four that the wise man lists. It is something that he does not understand!

So, I come to this part of the narrative with a sense of wonder, appreciating the breath-taking beauty of being attracted to one particular young woman and yet the sheer mystery of the chemistry that binds you to another soul. Her name was, Jean Perkins. How did she come into my orbit of attention?

Jean Perkins

Perkins Family
First Row: Jean, Edgar, Maggie, Ronnie
Second Row: Muriel, Audrey, David

Jean lived in Llanarthney; was born on November 14th, 1942, and was the third of five children, born to Edgar and Margaret Perkins. Her siblings were Audrey, David, Muriel and Ronnie. They lived just beneath Middleton Hall, [which is now 'The National Botanic Garden of Wales'] in a house that had a small holding and a field, where they had cows for milking.

Jean doing her farming work with Daisy the cow!

The parents were godly and committed to honouring the Lord Jesus, knowing him as their Lord and Saviour. They attended the Gospel Hall in Blue Street, Carmarthen and were key, active members of the Church. The church would have been seen as 'Open Brethren'. The children brought up in this home, also committed their lives to Christ, and so when I came to know Jean, she was already a devout Christian.

My first introduction was when I went with my Father when he was preaching at the Hall. I was around 9 years of age at the time, and the Perkins family were there. I would have been too shy and too young at the time to take much notice of the Perkin's girls, but Jean's memory of that visit was that I smiled like a 'Cheshire cat'.

In the mid-teens Jean became friendly with my sister and this gave me the opportunity of getting to know her. We also were involved with a Christian holiday camp, organised by Mr Beale of Swansea. We went to Tavistock one year, and on another occasion to Yeovil. These were ideal times to get to know other young people and it resulted in many courtships and eventually marriages.

Summer Holiday Bible Camp [1962]

I suspect, I was very slow off the mark for although I was attracted to this beautiful young lady, I was beaten to it by one of my friends. That is how it stood for many months until I heard that they had 'split-up'. This time, I was not going to allow the opportunity, if there was any possibility of it, to pass me bye. Jean is a vivacious person, well turned out, attractive and fun to be with. She was fully committed to Christ; we shared so much common interests. She worked as Secretary to the Clerk of Carmarthenshire District Council, and took the minutes of the council meetings.

Jean and David [1963]

I would have been around 19 years of age, when Jean was in our home in Penygroes and I offered to take her home on my Lambretta scooter. This was my opportunity. In response to a question from Jean as to whether I would be coming down to the Saturday evening Bible teaching meeting, next Saturday, I responded with the word - perhaps?

Back came her response - 'Perhaps what'? I then plucked up the courage to say, provided I can take you out afterwards and back came the words I wanted to hear, 'Of, course you can'. That ride back from Llanarthney to Penygroes, was like travelling on a heavenly chariot, my heart was full of joy and my spirit light hearted.

Here are a few details that are a sequel to that story. The preacher that Saturday evening was Mr D R Roberts from Evangelistic Hall, Llanelli. He spoke to me after the service and said, "*Why are you here tonight, David*". Back came the reply, "*To hear you, Mr Roberts!*". To this day I repent of that white lie.

After the service I took Jean to a restaurant, which was rather a posh name for a 'fish and chips' bar. While, we were enjoying our meal together, who came in were many of the church friends that we normally mixed with. I thought that I had selected a place that would have given us some anonymity, but our cover was blown on our first date, and news was out: "Jean Perkins is courting David Rees". I put it that way round, because Jean was the news. She was very attractive to the men!

Jean's first visit to my home after we had started dating was somewhat inauspicious. I picked her up in my Lambretta. It was a damp evening, with drizzly rain. The road from her home was narrow, and we had to drive across a narrow bridge. As we were crossing, a Post Office van came towards us. I knew, that if I braked then my scooter would have skidded into the van. So, I kept going, moving as close to the edge as possible, only for my 'kick starter' peddle to hit the van's rear wheel as we came off the bridge, and we were pushed into the hedge. Jean, had dressed for the occasion, in a coat that was a beautiful delicate shade of light pink. The coat was never the same after this incident, it was covered in mud! So, when we arrived at 93, Waterloo Rd, Jean's first stop was the bathroom to clean up.

Morris 8, ready to be cleaned by Jean and my sister, Ann. Parked outside 93 Waterloo Rd, Penygroes.

It was not soon after this that I transitioned from a scooter to a car. We had a number of closed run incidents on the scooter, including coming off it on a frozen road during a dark winter journey. Also, I had to leave the scooter in a number of places because the two-stroke engine was cutting out. It took me a while to work out that the problem was Jean's dress, it was blocking the intake of air! At this time Jean wouldn't wear trousers, because it was a man's attire! So, shortly afterwards I bought a Morris 8, which I was particularly proud of.

On another occasion, when I was driving my Morris 8, along the Mumbles Road, with Jean in the passenger seat a police car overtook us and flashed us to stop. I stopped and he came to the driver's window saying: "*Young man, your driving is not up to much, you were waving all over the road, have you been drinking?*". To which I replied: "*No, I don't drink alcohol*". Then there was a pause, and he looked over at Jean and said: "*I can see what your problem is, you are being distracted by a lovely young lady, be more careful in future*" and he walked away.

Our relationship blossomed, and two years later we got married at Ebenezer Gospel Hall on the 24th September, 1965. The wedding ceremony was conducted by Mr David Lawrence, who was one of the elders of the church and my best-man was Michael Stephens from Pantaffynon.

'24th September, 1965, Wedding Day at Ebenezer Gospel Hall, Carmarthen
[Peter, Nesta, Mark, Lewis, David, Jean, Sian, Ann, Dylan, Rhoda, Graham]
[Note: The wedding was on a Friday - John was not able to attend]

We went on our honeymoon to Boscombe and stayed at a Christian hotel. That was a mistake, because we met a couple there from Swansea, Sylvanus Taylor and his wife, Margaret, who knew us. So, our cover was blown, our first day as man and wife revealed! However, it was not without recompense, because at the end of the week they gave us a lovely wedding present.

9

'ALL THINGS' PERKINS

You have seen from the preceding chapter how a Perkins has become a Rees. The Perkins family originally hailed from Maesybont and surrounding area, certainly those belonging to the last five generations of Jean's family. Appendix III gives the family tree of the Perkins family.

One of Jean's relatives was Sidney Perkins. After military service with the Royal Artillery, he became a teacher and then a Headmaster of a School in Barry. Sidney had a long-term interest in the history of Gelli Aur area and produced a number of maps, one of which is shown. At the centre of the map is Hebron, the church built by the Perkins family.

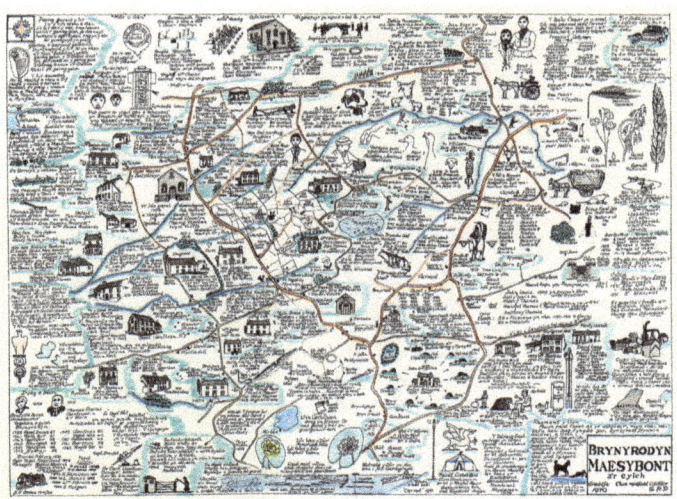

Sidney Perkins map of the Maesybont/Gelli Aur area.

Richard Perkins

Jean's grandfather was Richard Perkins, who we have already met in an earlier chapter. He was the market gardener that sold produce to my mother Mrs Mary Rees. The story of the spiritual history of the family begins with Richard.

Richard Perkins and family [1918]

This is young Richard Perkins with his wife, Sarah Ann and their four children. The youngest is Edgar, sitting in his Mum's lap, and he is the father of my wife Jean.

Then there are two daughters, Margaret and Agnes, being held by Dad. The family had another addition, Amelia.

The eldest son is David, who was tragically killed in WW2. He went down with HMS Neptune, on the 19th Dec, 1941 when the battleship hit an unchartered minefield in the Mediterranean, off Tripoli.

Richard, Sarah and Richard's brother, David were converted after the 1904 revival and they were fully persuaded that they had been saved by God's grace. Nothing would move them from that. They were saved people and committed to preaching the gospel in the open-air. There is an entry in Richard Perkins diary for the 25 May, 1929, worth quoting. They were in Llandeilo:

"Election candidates speaking after which we went to give testimony, but Chief Philips refused us to do so, because he said the people were blocking the traffic, whereas he stood and looked on for an hour on the crowds blocking the traffic while the Tories spoke. My brother told him he was a respecter of persons, and we moved from our usual place, because of his command. May God forgive him and have mercy on his soul!"

Cefnberrach Calvinistic Methodist Chapel

The family attended Cefnberrach Calvinistic Methodist Chapel. The church came into existence following a secret base for the Nonconformists in the Golden Grove area around 1700 which were visited by notable preachers, like, Daniel Rowlands, and William Williams, Pantycelin.[10,11] These were Gospel men and the consequence was the building of a new chapel in Cefnberrach [1747].

By the beginning of the 20th century, sadly the chapel had lost its gospel cutting edge and had become more of a social enterprise. The minister was noted for being a liberal in terms of his Christian convictions. This resulted in tension, between those in the congregation who were 'saved' and those who believed that you could not have that kind of certainty. That would have been the position that the minister would have taken. The Perkins family however were strong in their convictions and made of firm stuff. The story goes, that when the minister preached something that was not in tune with the gospel, there would come a voice from the congregation; it would be the voice of Richard Perkins, saying "Mae'r ceiliog yn canu!" ["The cock is crowing"!].

Hebron Neuadd Efengylu

Clearly this could not continue, and it resulted in 'Hebron', Neuadd Efengylu being built in 1923 by the two Perkins brothers, Richard and David. The literal translation of 'Neuadd Efengulu' is Halls for evangelising.

Hebron – pic taken at the funeral of Jim Jones, Martha's husband. This was the last service at the chapel - Saturday, April 12th, 2014.

There were a number of churches built around this time which had a similar ethos – they were churches that were committed to proclaiming the gospel. Eglwys Efengyledd, Penygroes [1910]; Evangelistic Hall, Tycroes [1932]. This was then followed by one in Cross Hands, and other places. These churches over the years have had a fruitful ministry.

My brother-in-law, Ronnie has written something about the history and impact of these churches which was published in the Welsh language. I have included an English translation of this article in Appendix II. It represents something of the rich Christian tradition that Jean and I have come from.

Richard Perkins passed away on Aug. 3rd, 1954 and Sarah Perkins on Feb. 4, 1971.

Edgar Perkins and Margaret Ann Perkins, nee Williams

As we have seen Edgar was brought up in a devout Christian home and embraced the faith of his family. Clearly, there was a point in his life when he came to a personal faith in Jesus Christ and this would have been when he was a child, around seven years of age. Margaret's experience was somewhat different as narrated by her daughter Jean.

"Margaret Ann Perkins (nee Williams) attended Llanddarog Church in Wales, which she had done from early childhood. As a young child with her two sisters, Rachel Mary, and Sarah Jane, she walked three times on a Sunday from their home in Pedairheol,

Porthyrhyd to Llanddarog Church. Their home was a religious home, where the church played a central part in their lives. They were taught the Bible in School as well as in the Church and learnt in Welsh and English large parts of it.

The Church Army – Llanddarog [1934]

When they were in their twenties, the Church Army had a mission at Llanddarog Church, and Margaret and Sarah attended the services. After hearing a clear gospel message one evening, as they were walking home, Margaret turned to Sarah and said "I've been saved". Sarah responded "So have I". So began her Christian life, where she had come through to a certain faith in the Lord Jesus, which sustained and strengthened her throughout her life. Margaret recalling that day, said 'The Lord saved me on the road home'."

Edgar was born at Ffynon Farm and spent his early years there. The farm was on Lord Cawdor's estate and one that they rented. The situation was idyllic, in an area of natural beauty, with such areas as 'Golwyg y Byd' [view of the world], Gelli Aur [Golden Grove] and a wonderful panoramic view of the Towy valley, including Dryslwyn and Dynever Castles.

The farm was a market garden and dairy farm. The children growing up had a lot of fun together. There is the story, of the day Uncle Albert called, when he asked if he could help. He was told: "Yes, you can - milk the cow at the end of the stall". He went, only to discover that the cow, was not a cow at all, but a bull! He was not amused.

Edgar and Margaret Perkins [1939]

Following Margaret's conversion, Edgar and Margaret started their courtship. They got introduced when Margaret was 'in service' in a house in Maesybont, and that was the beginning of their relationship which blossomed and continued to the end of their lives. They got married on Nov. 28th, 1939.

The two became five within just over three years of married life and eventually they became seven.

Audrey, Margaret, Jean, Edgar, David [1943]

The Perkins family – Silver Wedding Anniversary [1964]. Edgar, Audrey, Ronnie, Jean, David, Muriel, Margaret

Edgar, was a farmer and a tradesman and finished his working life with Carmarthenshire District Council. He was also a keen gardener but his primary commitment was the interest of God's kingdom. He was regularly seen on a Saturday in Carmarthen town, carrying a gospel text banner, with his brother-in-law, Jim Jones and giving out gospel literature. He was faithful to the end. He was a key leader at Ebenezer Gospel Hall.

Golden Wedding Anniversary [1989]

Margaret ably supported Edgar in his work and also in discharging his Christian responsibilities. The home was a place where visiting preachers and missionaries were entertained and stayed.

She was devoted to the Lord and was an exceptionally hard worker, bringing up the family with limited resources. She managed the household and the finances well, was articulate but could occasionally be outspoken. At least you knew what she thought.

As one who married into the family, I learned to appreciate what a great woman she was, with godly priorities.

Edgar was gentle and placid, but totally resolute in terms of his convictions. He was a wonderful example of Christian faithfulness and godliness.

He went to be with his Lord, on April 17th, 2001 and was interned at Hebron, Maesybont. That occasion is captured by one of his grandsons, Rev. Stephen Rees, which he wrote about in Christchurch Easter Magazine, Little Heath, April, 2007. I will quote it verbatim:

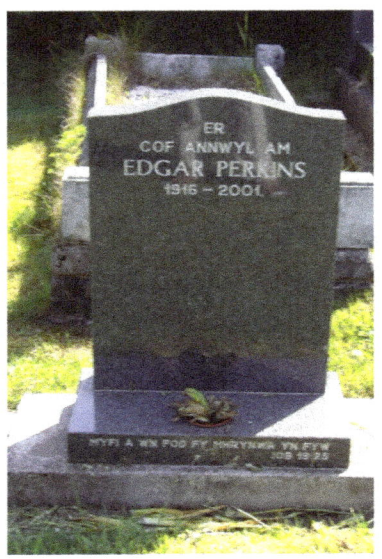

"One of the most memorable funerals I have been to was my Grandfather's. His name was Edgar Perkins; he had been a farmer and a builder, had brought up five children and was a wonderful Christian man. He loved the Lord Jesus and wherever he went he would give out leaflets to people explaining who Jesus was and why he had come. On a Saturday morning and on Market day he would carry a banner with verses from the Bible on them around his home town of Carmarthen, in West Wales. He was a fearless follower of Jesus his Lord and Saviour. His desire was that many more people would experience with him the joy of sins forgiven and the hope of a home in heaven. Many people gathered for his burial.

It took place in the grounds of a small chapel in Maesybont. This chapel was built by my Great Grandfather and has many relatives buried there. It was a sunny spring day, and I stood with my family singing in Welsh and then listening to the triumphant words of Paul from 1 Cor. 15 being read in Welsh. It was a deeply moving occasion. It was a moment of great hope. Yes, we mourned the loss of our Grandfather, it was upsetting to see his widow standing alone at the side of his grave and yet as we heard the truths of the resurrection being read out, they lifted our hearts."

Some three years after her husband Edgar died, Margaret had a stroke which left her immobile. This was in 2004. This meant that she had to be placed in care and went to Plas y Dderwn Care Home, Johnstown, Carmarthen. She was well cared for and was contented in Christ. She was regularly visited by the family, with Jean making a weekly visit from Cardiff. Margaret went to be with the Lord, on Sunday, September 7th, 2008. There are many stories relating to Margaret that could be rehearsed because she was a remarkable character and very feisty, despite suffering a little dementia. I will give you two.

Story 1 On this particular day, when Jean was visiting, her Mum became quite emotional saying that there was a time when she didn't love everyone, but now she could say that she did. Well, she was instantly put to the test as Fred came in on his electric wheelchair, shouting 'Maggie, Maggie, Maggie'. Margaret turned to Jean and said with a fair amount of indignation: "I can't stand that man"! It turned out that Fred had asked Margaret to marry him, but she had said: "Not yet".

Story 2 When Margaret died, Audrey and her husband John, and David were there and to their surprise they heard the carer singing: "God is still on the throne, and he will remember his own". They asked, "How do you know that?". Back came the reply, "We could not but learn it, because Maggie was always singing it". What a wonderful testimony to the faith of an old lady.

Irelian Jones

Before I conclude this section, I want to return to one person we have already met, Irelian Jones. He was inextricably linked to Maesybont and to Hebron Hall, although he was not a Perkins. He was a multi-talented engineering man at the local quarry. He was technically and intellectually gifted, very much a gadget man – he invented breathalysers before they were ever thought about!

He adapted a van so he could take it around the villages of Wales and preach the gospel. He made it into a mobile home and sadly that led to a tragedy, for on one of these missions, he died through carbon monoxide poisoning. That day lives in my memory, because his funeral coincided with the marriage of my brother-in-law, David to Adelle. It was the 12th Oct, 1974. Such was the respect he was held in, my father-in-law Edgar and my brother in law, Ronnie, missed the reception in order to attend the funeral.

Jean Perkins' Siblings and Partners

Audrey and John Lloyd. Wedding, 13th Aug, 1981 – Hebron, Maesybont. Offspring: David John [28/7/1983]

David [deceased] and Adelle Beynon [with Paul and Andrew]. Wedding, 12th Oct, 1974 – Caersalem, Llanelli. Offspring: Helen Elizabeth [12/11/1977] Emma Mair [28/2/1981]

Muriel and Andrew Brown, Jan. 16th , 1988 – Ebenezer Gospel Hall, Carmarthen.

Ronnie and Joyce Evans[deceased], wedding, Sept 16th, 1978, Calfaria Chapel, Garnant. Offspring: Eifion Cynddylan [13/6/1981] Meleri Anwen [13/8/1979]

The next generation of Edgar Perkins family have made and are making a significant contribution to the work of God's kingdom, which I will now briefly summarise.

1. John and Audrey were both teachers before their retirement. Audrey was a primary school teacher and John a geography teacher. He broadened his area of expertise to embrace a whole range of disciplines in order to teach children who were in hospital for extended periods. When they got married, they lived in Ruabon in North Wales, but on John's retirement and when circumstances permitted, they relocated to Carmarthen in June 2002, to provide support for her

mother, who was now widowed. This was a great blessing to the family, as well as to the Ebenezer church family. John is now serving as an elder, secretary and Bible teacher at the fellowship. Their home over many years has been a conduit of hospitality to visiting preachers, holiday guests who visit Carmarthen and church members.

2. Ronnie was a librarian before retirement and Joyce a manager in the social services. On early retirement, mainly through poor eyesight, Ronnie managed the Bible bookshop at Ammanford market. Ronnie has always had a great love of books and nothing delights him more than engaging with the spiritual giants of the past. He was active as a lay preacher, fluent in both Welsh and English, before his eyesight limited this activity. Joyce entered her eternal rest on August 3rd, 2015 after suffering many years of respiratory ill health.

3. David, the eldest son was employed in the local authority health department as an administrator. Of all the Perkins children, David was the most practical, who could turn his hand to most things, like car maintenance, practical house maintenance and gardening. He looked after his parents with great love and diligence ensuring that their needs were always met, whether the car needed to pass the MOT or they required transport. When they had to give up driving, David would transport them to the fellowship meetings, whenever that was necessary. Adelle was a great support to him in this ministry. David passed away on June 23rd, 2018, having fought over a number of years a brave battle against leukaemia.

4. Muriel's husband, Andrew has put his Classics scholarship to good use by publishing extensively on Erasmus, producing his annotated edition of Erasmus' *Novum* Testamentum (the New Testament in Greek and Latin) which forms one section

of the international project to produce a new edition of Erasmus complete works. He has also published works on Robert Ferrar[12], the reformation Bishop and martyr in Wales and William Tyndale[13].

5. Eifion Cynddylan, is the only offspring of Richard Perkins family that continues the Perkins name. He also takes forward to the next generation the evangelical preaching and Christian heritage of the family as he is the minister at Noddfa Evangelical Church in Pontardulais. He is married to Suzanne, and they have two children, Josiah and Phoebe.

10

EARLY MARRIED LIFE – SWANSEA

Living in the Uplands meant that we were conveniently placed for the University. We were able to walk through Brynmill and Singleton Park to get to the University campus. If it was particularly wet, we travelled in by car.

Swansea Bay – Perspective from Dylan Thomas childhood home in the Uplands.
[Watercolour painting in our home – a gift from Stephen & Jenny on my 60th, birthday.]

I was at this time about to start the second year of my degree, and through my brother Peter's contacts we rented a furnished flat in the Uplands of Swansea. Jean, by this time had obtained a job as secretary to Prof. Street, the Head of Biology at the University. The Uplands was very much Dylan Thomas country, as his childhood home was not far from our flat. The watercolour painting gives the view of Swansea Bay, from the perspective of his childhood home

We made our spiritual home, Dunvant Gospel Hall, which is now called 'Dunvant Christian Fellowship'. It is now a vibrant, gospel centred, family and community orientated church with some of its key leaders, grandsons of the leading elder when we were members, a Mr Ernest Davies. [Phil Davies is now their Pastor, one of the grandsons].

The church in the 1960's was gospel centred but very conventional and committed to what were referred to as New Testament church practice principles. It was a warm-hearted fellowship but would have been seen as very conservative and very strict. This fitted our background but given the benefit of hindsight proved somewhat restrictive and inhibitive in terms of embracing more wholeheartedly a wider evangelical fraternity. This in part contributed to us not involving ourselves in parachurch organisations but rather committing ourselves to the local church. Looking back at this decision I feel that we missed out on the opportunities that University life offered in terms of witness, evangelism and fellowship.

Ernest Davies was a deeply spiritual man, a perfect gentleman with a gracious spirit and a deep love for God's people and God's word. He never imposed his convictions on others. He operated on the basis of *"Has thou faith? Have it to thyself before God"* [Romans 14:22 - KJV], a verse that he often quoted.

One family that were particularly kind to us was John and Sheila Davies. John was the son of Mr & Mrs Ernest Davies. They eventually had six sons, all of them committed Christians and two of them are now in full time Christian ministry [Mark and Phil]. They served the Lord with total abandon. There was one occasion that stands out in my memory, when John whispered in my ear, before the start of the service. Pray for me, I have bought a bus for the Sunday School and I have to tell the elders about it. True enough, he had bought a bus and often we would see John under the bus on the Sunday, sorting something out, in the best of his Sunday wears. They had a real passion for people and children, and John would be involved on a weekly basis in open-air preaching using the Swansea mobile unit [a van adapted for open-air preaching with loud speakers and a turn table].

Tom and Chall. Summerall, Swansea

Another couple that we got to know very well was Mr & Mrs Tom Summerall; they lived in the Uplands, they had no children and we often brought them to the fellowship in our car. Mr Summerall had a great knowledge of the scripture, very much into the Old Testament, in terms of its 'types and shadows' and allegorical teaching. He had been moulded by much of the London party exclusive teaching, and consequently, controversy regarding the eternal Sonship of Christ often followed him.

Looking back on this time, on mature reflection we sense that we came too much under their influence. On the one hand they were a blessing to us, but on the other hand it could be somewhat stifling. They were very kind to us in their will; they left us a small legacy. There are a number of memories concerning Tom and Chall, as she was referred to that are worth sharing.

We often were invited to their house for refreshments after the Sunday evening service. Tom would always give thanks before we ate and 'Chall' would grab the nearest thing to put on her head before Tom prayed. Often it would be the tea cosy. A head covering was sacrosanct. That was a sight to behold!

Mr Summeral's capacity to speak on the Bible was legendary. There was an occasion some years later when they were on holiday with us. We were attending a church in Stevenage. I was leading a Bible study, which I introduced and out of politeness I invited Mr Summerall to make a contribution. He had no notes. He did contribute and when he had finished, three quarters of an hour later, the time had gone and we had come to the end of our "conversational Bible reading"!

On another occasion, they visited us when we lived in Cardiff. By that time, we had two children and we had bought a television. The Summerall's would have been deeply disappointed and even possibly offended if they knew that we had brought 'the world into our home'. The fact was we could hide the television without any difficulty, but what about the aerial? That surely was a real visible tell-tale sign of spiritual declension. Well, I resolved that problem by going up on the roof of the house and pulling the aerial down.

When they arrived and came out of the car, I could see that all of my effort was totally unnecessary. Mr Summerall was very bent and was not able to lift his head, so he would not have seen the aerial in any case. There was a consequence to my stupidity. It took me a long time to put the aerial back and reposition it to give the best signal reception.

11

SPREADING OUR WINGS

Welwyn Garden City

Graduating led to opportunities. Surveying a number of options, I made the decision to accept a job opportunity with Imperial Chemical Industries Ltd. This was as a technical officer in the Plastics Division which was based at Welwyn Garden City [WGC]. I joined on 10th July, 1967 and became a member of a team in the Computer Techniques section of the Engineering Department.

The prime activity of the group was to develop real-time computer control software for implementation in various manufacturing plants. One was an ethylene manufacturing process in Teesside. This was an essential ingredient in the production of plastics. The computer that we worked on was an IBM 1800 real-time process control computer. Whilst IBM had produced real-time software for this computer, ICI policy was always to strike out independently and develop its own particular algorithms, to have a measure of secrecy over its manufacturing process. I recall an occasion when there was a Chinese delegation who were visiting the plant to obtain a manufacturing licence on the process. The technology that ICI were going to licence was the old technology, the plant that we were working on was the new technology, so they made sure that the new plant was completely covered and shielded from the eyes of the delegation.

Another problem that I worked on was a batch process based in the Wirral. I developed a simulation model for the CORVIC process, explored ways of making the process more productive and therefore more cost efficient. Since the manufacturing plants were away from Welwyn, this meant quite a lot of travelling, particularly to Teesside, often on an overnight sleeper train or occasionally flying.

Moving away from Wales, had its challenges, not least where were we going to live? Welwyn Garden City, is a beautifully designed new town, green and leafy, that was built as a dormitory area for people working in London. As part of my job appointment, we had the opportunity of a renting a maisonette not far from the Company, which clearly, we took. At that time, we had no means of buying our own property. Also, we were able to rent a house, when our family started to expand. Since there was a number of weeks between starting my job and the maisonette being available, we were very kindly provided accommodation by Glyn and Eirona Davies, in Harlow. Glyn is the brother of John Davies of Dunvant. Their son Stephen and his wife, Gill are now missionaries out in Dar es Salaam, Tanzania.

Ceramic Panel - Witold Stefan

One of the blessings of living in the Maisonette was meeting a ceramic painter, Witold Stefan, from Krakow, Poland who lived in the same block of flats. He very kindly gave us one of his ceramic panels.

After two years, the Company asked me to move up to Teesside and that was the point when I reassessed my career choices. Primarily, for family reasons I decided to pursue a career in academia and that door opened for me, with my first appointment as a lecturer at Hendon College of Technology. This is now part of Middlesex University. I commenced on 1st September, 1969.

We decided at the time we joined ICI, that this was the time to think about starting a family and so Jean did not pursue any secular employment. On the 9th May, 1968 we had the blessing of our first son, Paul Lewis.

Paul with Joan Patterson [1968]

This was a very eventful occasion at a number of levels. We had made a number of friends, and despite Jean being 'heavy with child' we had gone on this Saturday evening to a Bible teaching event at Ealing with Joan Patterson, who was a matron at the Queen Elizabeth II Hospital, in WGC. During the service, Jean' waters broke and so we were faced with rushing back, along the North circular to get to QEII hospital. I was in a bit of a state, and lost my way in the process, which did not help our situation. Well it turned out Paul was a long time coming, in fact Jean was in labour for 4 days, and when he did come, he had to be put into an incubator because he had swallowed some fluids.

I failed on a number of counts. Jean requested some light reading, she had in mind a 'Women's Weekly' but I took a missionary book 'Life amongst the Savage Tribes'! When I saw her after the birth, I said in a light hearted way, 'a girl next time, love' and Jean subsequent response was that if she had a shot gun, I would have been dead, because of the difficult time she had experienced. I then proceeded to take a photograph, only to discover that I had forgotten to put a film in my camera! These were a catalogue of disasters. The only slip up Jean made was to tell someone who came to visit her, that the baby was in an incinerator!

Pat & Brian Davies, Jean, Ruth Davies, Paul [1969]

We had a number of friends, which were based in London and we frequently met on a Friday evening for fellowship and Bible studies. There was Brian and Pat Davies, who originally were from Llanelli. Brian, was a headmaster of a primary School. Then there was Colin and Val Lacey, both Londoners and a cockney, who we referred to as 'Brother Bannocks'. It is worth noting, that two of the group became popular Bible conference speakers, Brian and Colin. Colin in terms of his style modelled himself on a well-known conference speaker, Albert Leckie.

In terms of Church fellowship, we attended Marley Chapel. This was an active fellowship committed to the gospel, but much different to the fellowship we had left. They were delightful people, but we would have benefitted if we had made a more gradual transition along the spectrum of traditions that we now were meeting. We had not been prepared well for it. There were a number of people who worked at ICI who were members of the church, one of them was John Hamilton. Living now in Edinburgh, we are in the same fellowship as one of his nephews, Derek Hamilton.

There are two memories that I want to record of Bible teaching we had at Marley Chapel. I recall the teaching by a Scotsman, David Haxton, on the offerings in Leviticus. It was memorable, he had the ability to make the subject live and to describe the pots, pans, brazen altar, the sacrifices etc in a way that connected with the heart and mind and pointed us to the Lord Jesus Christ. Another memory was John Riddle's addresses on the Saviours, God had sent to Israel, during the time of the Judges, and how they pointed to the greater Saviour that God sent in the person of his Son, the Lord Jesus.

Given our ambivalence about certain developments at Marley Chapel, we decided to go and help a small church in Stevenage, which was struggling. This turned out to be somewhat short lived, as I decided to change job and with it change where we lived.

Luton

Changing employment meant the opportunity to think about where we should live. The decision was made that Luton would be a good place to buy a house. Prices were more reasonable than at WGC and also it was a direct route to Hendon, travelling down the M1 motorway. Another attraction, was a Church at Onslow Road. We had a number of good friends there who shared the same church convictions and so, we bought a semi-detached house at Sundon Park in Luton. This became our home, but we didn't realise at that stage how short lived our stay would be.

On January 13th, 1970 our second son, Stephen Philip. was born at the hospital in Luton. Another great blessing in our lives. Unlike Paul's birth, his was pretty instantaneous, borrowing the words of the midwives, 'Shiphrah and Puah' [Ex. 1:19], his was 'lively' and that has characterised his personality ever since!

Jean with Stephen [1970]

We became great friends with Ian & Janette Grant and we have remained friends, ever since. We shared many holidays together. They currently live in Aberdeen.

Ian and Janette Grant, Jean with Stephen, Paul, Ruth, Fiona and Helen. Holiday in New Forest National Park – 1970.

The church had acquired a reputation for being a good Bible teaching church, and it had a strong following for a monthly teaching programme which had a Bible class format. They invited accredited Bible teachers and the events were very stimulating, if not sometimes controversial, with some of the contributions coming from the congregation. The leading elder was a saintly man by the name of Tom Garrett. He had a very ordinary job, but a great knowledge of the scriptures and a deep love for the Lord.

He had strong views and could be quite uncompromising if a perspective was expressed that he was not in sympathy with.

There are a couple of memories that I want to share. The first was a special weekend, when we had a visiting preacher, John Glenville, who came from an actor family. It was the weekend when there were power cuts because of the miner's strike. So we met on the Sunday evening using candlelight. That was an occasion for a preacher like Mr Glenville to excel. He was a moving, elasticated, morphed body, his head disappearing behind the pulpit, then reappearing with his hands raised against candlelight shadows. It was surreal. His subject was the Lord coming in salvation and judgement. The combination of theme and circumstances, added a definite poignancy to the whole evening.

The second, was the funeral of Mr Pinner. It was taken by Peter Feban. This was the first funeral service he had taken and he was a little nervous. After an opening scripture reading, he proceeded to ask, Mr Pinner to pray. At that point, my friend Ian Grant, whispered, "Keep an eye on that coffin!"

During my first year at Hendon College a Senior Lecturer's post in Control Engineering, was advertised in the School of Electrical and Electronic Engineering at the Polytechnic of Wales. I saw this as an opportunity to return to Wales and although I knew that it was a big hurdle to jump, I nevertheless had peace about making the application. I was appointed to the post and became one of the youngest academics at the Polytechnic to be a Senior Lecturer [SL] in Electrical Engineering. I commenced on 1st September, 1970. This ruffled the feathers of some of my colleagues but these were somewhat becalmed when the lecturing union, shortly after my appointment, negotiated a national new unified pay scale which allowed staff, who met certain criteria, to transition through the SL barrier.

My one year at Hendon was not a wasted year, however, because my subject leader was an able control lecturer, John Hargreaves, and I learned a lot from him. He did however have the reputation of spending more time off-campus than on-campus.

This decision to return to Wales provided the immediate challenge of putting our house up for sale, which we had only just bought. In order to minimise our costs, we decided not to use an Estate agent but try and market the house ourselves. We managed to do this but it was not without experiencing something of an emotional rollercoaster.

The first interested customer was an American. They wanted to buy the house and so Jean rang me up at work to say that we had sold the house. We celebrated by taking Ian & Janette Grant down to London and treating them to a meal. We never saw the American again!

The second person was an Irishman, who ran his own building site clearance haulage Company in London. He wanted to buy the property and was ready there and then to give us cash in hand. We refused to accept that and insisted we would do it legally correct through a solicitor. That was set in motion, but then around a week later I had a phone call from Jean, saying that workmen were in the house putting in storage heaters. My immediate response was, *"You didn't leave them in, did you?"*. Well, Jean had and when I came home from work the heaters had been installed. In the end, everything worked out well, the house was sold and we were free to move back to Wales. The Grant's very kindly provided accommodation to us for our two last weeks in Luton, because we had to move out of our house early.

12

COMING HOME

Pontypridd and Life. Home for us now was Pontypridd, which is at the mouth of two major valleys, the Rhondda and Merthyr.

Famous Bridge over the River Taff Pontypridd

It is the County town of Rhondda Cynon Taff. The reputation and wealth of the Town was based on the Coal industry, but by the 1970's that was a quickly diminishing industry in the County. The Polytechnic, was historically the School of Mines but by the 1970's the mining department was a shadow of its former self and within a decade it was amalgamated into the School of Chemical Engineering.

We decided to buy a new detached house on the Common in Pontypridd, which was still being built. This meant that we had to rent a house from the Council. They placed us on the Rhydyfelin Estate in a terraced town house. This happened remarkably seamlessly, which we were pleasantly surprised by, but we soon discovered that things were not quite as they appeared to be.

It turned out that our next-door neighbour was a young mother with three children and was a person with a bad reputation; she was very much a lady of the night! Many of her previous neighbours had come and gone very quickly, so it was a house that the council had found difficult to let. We knew that this would only be a temporary residence for us, so we put up with some abnormal behavioural patterns. One day, Jean had left some clothes for drying on the line in the garden overnight. Her underwear, my underwear and some other things. By the morning they had all disappeared, nothing left. We had our suspicions, but no evidence.

The months went by, Christmas came and Jean had compassion on the children and bought them boxes of sweets. On Christmas Eve, we heard a noise of something been put through our letter box. We could not believe our eyes, there on the floor was one of my briefs, very discoloured and extended. Clearly, Jean's compassion had touched some emotion of guilt! On the day we moved, we were royally complemented by our neighbour with the words: "You are the best b..... neighbours I have ever had".

Moving to Wingfield Close, in the Commons, was a great relief and blessing. The house was in an elevated location with a lounge view overlooking the valley going out from Pontypridd to Ynysybwl, and far below us were terraces of houses. This was a glorious perspective. The down side of this was that both our front and back garden were on a slope, and this required a lot of landscaping.

It was in Pontypridd that we purchased our first television. We had resisted it up to now, but with the children spending time watching television with a very kind neighbour, Mr and Mrs Godwin, we decided that this was a bullet we had to bite. That decision was accelerated when one of the children quoted Mrs Godwin as saying, "*When Dad has enough money, he will buy you a television*". My memory of what I first enjoyed watching was the 'The world at War' series, a documentary on the second world war. This we thought was a powerful documentary.

Jean with Stephen [1971]

Having spent around 6 months living in terraced housing, meant that the children, who were still young had not settled into a helpful rhythm of sleep. Any noise and Jean used to pick them up because she didn't want to disturb the neighbours. We therefore resolved that once we moved into our new home that this was a problem we would sort out. We made that decision, on a beautiful Summer evening when the bedroom window was slightly open, that we would not pick the children up. We would leave them cry until they fell asleep. And that is exactly what we did.

However, at 11 pm, there was a ring on the door bell and there stood a policeman. He was responding to a complaint from one of the houses down the valley, that a child was in distress. So, Jean brought this healthy, bonnie baby and the PC officer was immediately satisfied that there was no issue of child neglect.

Living on the Common, seemed to turn the clock back in time. The garden was an ideal place to play 'Indians'.

Stephen and Paul [1971] in our back garden.

Also, the local farmer looked as if he was from another era. He arrived on his horse and cart asking whether he could deliver us milk. We said yes, and we purchased some milk, only to learn that drinking it was something of a challenge. It carried the taste of the farm, so the next time he called, we said we wouldn't want him to continue delivering. His response was "What is the matter boy, if it is too strong for you, then I can dilute it, no problem there!" We weren't persuaded.

There was one occasion when disaster nearly struck. Jean was in Ynysangharad Park, which had a pool. Stephen was in the pushchair and Paul, was holding her hand. She was momentarily distracted; Paul had disappeared and she could not see him anywhere. The next thing she saw was a man, with his trousers soaked, carrying a drenched Paul in his arms. He had fallen into the pool, and this man had seen what happened and went in to rescue him. Jean was so shocked; she didn't think that she had time to thank the man before he had disappeared. Here was an unnamed angel who carried out a great rescue. Here is another act of God's providence.

Polytechnic of Wales

I settled into academic life at the Polytechnic with reasonable ease. The Department was preparing for its accreditation to deliver an Honours degree. Up to now, it offered a Higher National Diploma [HND] and a College Associateship [CA] which was accepted by the Institution of Electrical and Electronic Engineering [IEE] as an entry qualification for Associate membership. The Head of Department was a Mr Morris Dummer and he belonged to the old school.

I remember once having the two-door treatment, which was the one to be avoided, but I never forgot it. I had set an examination paper where in two separate questions I had spelt the word Nyquist incorrectly [spelt it as 'Nuquist']. I can see even now his finger pointing to the word, "*What is this?*", and then after a pause, his finger went to another question, "*What is this?*".

Staff and students [CA] - POW, Department of EE
[FR – Morris Dummer [4], Bill Lambert [5], TR – Colin Smith [1],
who became a lifelong friend]

There was an iciness in the tone, the point was made and never forgotten. After that, I was never casual about my checking of examination questions. Despite this put down, he could also be encouraging, for example by saying that the expertise I brought to the School represented its future.

In 1972, I became a Member of the Institution of Electrical Engineers [MIEE] and I became a Chartered Engineer on the 6th May, 1974 [CEng]. I was also in the same year [1972], given the opportunity to register for a PhD with the Council of National Awards [CNAA]. A number of younger members of staff were also encouraged to do this to raise the intellectual quotient of the Department. I was given remission on my teaching timetable of 1 day a week, and worked through my vacations on my research, apart from family holidays. I remember one eureka moment, I was lying on my bed, half asleep, when an idea came to my mind and I immediately got up and went into College at around 2:0 am to test the hypothesis on the hybrid computer.

My line manager was Bill Lambert and that represented a different challenge. He was the subject leader in Control Engineering, an able academic but a little insecure.

David Rees – Sketch by Bill Lambert [1981]

He had been working for a higher degree for a number of years on non-linear optimizing algorithms, using hybrid computer techniques, but never somehow landed the plane. Sadly, Bill took his own life in 1981. His marriage was in difficulties at the time and he became a Warden of the first student residential Hall at the College. It was at this time that he died. He had taken an interest in sketching and he made a sketch of me in 1981.

Church Fellowship.

When we lived at Pontypridd, we fellowshipped at Treforest Gospel Hall, which was not far from the Polytechnic Campus. It was an elderly church, with about 30 members. They were very warm hearted, caring and delighted to have a young family joining them.

The leading elder was Mr Gay. He and his wife showed us considerable kindness. Mrs Gay was very gracious, perspicacious lady. She saw in Paul and Stephen qualities, that we as parents would have been oblivious of. She felt that there was something special about them and that the Lord would set them apart for some aspect of Christian ministry. She was right and that will be covered in the 'Shoots' section of these memoirs.

Mr & Mrs Gay, Paul and Stephen
1972 – Brecon Beacons

Another, family that were particularly helpful were Mr and Mrs Langham. Mr Langham was a music teacher, and Mrs Langham was his second wife. His first had died. It was a fascinating relationship to observe, and gave an insight into the adoration that sometimes comes from the second wife! Mr Langham was a book man and had a big theological library. He frequently spoke at Church, and invariable his wife would say to him in imperfect English, "Cliff, you 'was' wonderful, Cliff, you 'was' wonderful". I must confess we didn't often share the same enthusiasm. Jean used to say that I would have to wait for my second wife to have that kind of adulation!

There are a few memories of eccentric visiting preachers. One was a Mr Thomas from Caerphilly, who had made his life work studying the minor prophets. His style was unique, he was like an accelerating train, who picked up momentum as he progressed through his study, his hands would be flaying, his body constantly moving, his material dense and he would invariably leave his congregation exhausted. By the time he had finished, they were desperate for Valium to calm the nerves!

Another occasion was the visit of a missionary from South America. His name was Mr Bradford and later he joined the charismatic 'Bradford Movement'. We provided accommodation for him and he hardly had been in the house a few minutes, before he sussed the location of the house and decided that it was ideal for an 'open-air' witness. Without requesting permission, he opened the front window, connected his loudspeaker and proceeded to preach using his microphone. I have no idea, what the people in the valley below thought. We knew what we felt, we were profoundly embarrassed and had been taken advantage of.

We were four years in fellowship at Treforest and the time came for us to reappraise where we saw our long-term future. We concluded that the fellowship was not the best place to bring up a family. There were no young people, or at least very few, and those that had come through the church, had either moved away or where not interested in Christianity. So, we decided, with considerable heart searching, that the time had come, for the sake of the family to move to Cardiff. It was a difficult decision to make and one that we committed to the Lord. We decided to try and open the door, in terms of buying a house in Cardiff and selling our own. It was at a difficult time in the housing market. Well, the door opened, without us feeling that we had to force it open. We were Cardiff bound.

13

PITCHING OUR TENT IN CARDIFF

When we moved to Cardiff, we had established a reputation by friends of being 'moving pillars' in the context of our church life. So, the expression 'pitching our tent' is an appropriate description in terms of this move, given our past history! It turned out however, to be the longest 'tent pitching' of our married life. We moved to Cardiff in the middle of September of 1974 and we left Cardiff in March, 2016.

2 Ceiriog Drive, Pantmawr CF14 7TU

The house we purchased was split-level and on a housing development in Pantmawr. This is located between Whitchurch and Rhiwbina and is in the North Cardiff constituency . This became our happy home for 42 years.

It was ideally situated for travelling to the Polytechnic and also close to Bethesda, the church that was our spiritual home for 42 years. It was also, conveniently placed for the city centre with easy access to the main road artery [M4], travelling either East or West.

Attractions of Cardiff
[tea-cloth in the kitchen]

The children settled in well, apart from an initial aberration in choice of School, when we put Paul in the Welsh medium language school in Cathays. It soon became apparent that this was not the best option for him and so we moved him to Rhiwbina Junior School. Stephen was not at the right age to start his schooling at that time.

The growth of Welsh medium schools is a fascinating development in Wales. They are seen as providing a good education standard, somewhat elitist in terms of the families that are attracted to such schools. They are also culturally relevant to Wales and the Welsh language. If a parent has aspirations for their child to work in the Welsh media, or even in Welsh politics then having this educational background has its advantages. The North Cardiff constituency, was not particularly Welsh when we moved into the area, but as the years have gone by it has become more Welsh.

Marjorie & Stuart Bateman

Living in Pantmawr were Marjorie and Stuart Bateman, who were members of Bethesda. They showed us great kindness from the start and we became good friends. Stuart was a civil servant working in the Welsh Office, and he was an elder of the church. He was a typical civil servant, always smartly dressed and articulate, linguistically precise. On the very first Sunday they invited us for Sunday lunch. Many years later, I had the privilege of taking both Stuart and Marjorie's funeral. Stuart passed away first, when he was 70, following a long decline through dementia. Marjorie some fifteen years later.

Ros & Stuart Gerrish [2009]

Another couple that we got to know well and who entertained us from the start were Ros and Stuart Gerrish and they become our lifelong friends. We have spent a number of holidays together, including going to Florida, and numerous Christian conferences like Word Alive and Keswick

Good friends from those early days are Colin & Meryl Williams. At that time, they lived in Canada, but we got to know them through their visits to Cardiff to see their parents. In recent years, they have lived in Cardiff where Colin was a Professor of Celtic Studies at Cardiff University. I mention Colin in my first chapter on his visit to Penygroes. He currently is at Cambridge University, although his home is still Cardiff.

Meryl & Colin Williams [2009]

Fire and our constituency MP

Our home was the second of three houses in a cul-de-sac – which later was expanded to five houses, after one of our neighbours bought some more land to expand his estate. This brings me to a story that is worth telling.

The houses on both our right and left, exchanged ownership fairly quickly, mainly through marriages failing. Within the space of five years there were four broken marriages. One of our new neighbours was Gwilym and Linda Jones and I am happy to say they are still together but now living in Lisvane.

Gwilym was a conservative Cardiff councillor, and in 1983 he was selected by them to fight the Cardiff North constituency, which he duly won on the 9th June, 1983. But it was not without some drama, because the press when the campaign was at its 'high noon', released the news that Gwilym, when he was a teenager had put fire to the headmaster's office at Whitchurch High School. As a result of this he spent some time in a special school for badly behaved boys! The drama of the announcement was heightened when people realised that the candidate for Plaid Cymru, Dr Williams, was the psychiatrist who had treated Gwilym, some years previously. Well, that was the story that was circulating.

He served as our MP until 1 May, 1997 when the seat was lost to Labour and at that time was Parliamentary Under Secretary in the Welsh Office. Paul and Stephen often did leafletting for Gwilym at election time. The boys had fun at Gwilym's expense. Whenever he lit a fire, they would shout out; "Keep an eye on Gwilym. He is lighting a fire"!

It was at this time that Gwilym and Linda, extended their garden so that they could put up a tent to entertain their local Conservative constituents. That was an event; barrels of beer were rolling down Ceiriog Drive. People turned up in their droves and on one occasion I discovered a 'blue rinsed hair' lady, parking her car in our drive and proceeded to walk away. I pointed out to her that she couldn't do that, as I wanted access to my drive, so I asked her to move her car. She was quite indignant at that. As a matter of record, Gwilym and Linda's daughter, Fay Jones, won the Brecon and Radnorshire constituency for the Conservatives in the landslide election victory of 2019.

Drugs and Drama

Another neighbour who lived directly opposite us, was an Inspector of Police, John Waite, who was in charge of the drugs squad in South Wales. One morning, as I was going to work, I noticed that a number of men were staking the property. The news broke later that week that the police had carried out a drug's raid on the property. It turned out that the only drugs they found was a small bit of dried out cannabis. There was no court case but nevertheless shortly afterwards John resigned from the police force.

He was also a keen amateur actor and was the Director of Rhiwbina Drama Society. Stephen around this time was about 7 years of age and John recruited him to play a part in one of the plays.

Rhiwbina Amateur Dramatics – Stephen in the centre. [1976]

Stephen was gifted and the feedback that came back was that no one could be taught the skills that he had; it was instinctive, natural with a superb sense of timing. It was not surprising therefore that Stephen went on to study English and drama at University.

At that time Stephen was involved with a number of plays but the point came when one of the plays was somewhat raunchy and so we withdrew him from the cast. That was the end of his involvement with Rhiwbina Dramatic Society.

Skid Rebuke

Another story relating to Stephen, is the occasion when we took Paul and Stephen to Gabalfa Baptist to hear Nicky Cruise, a converted drugs dealer from the Bronx, New York. It was a winter, cold, icy evening in December and as we were travelling up Rhiwbina Hill, just past the Deri, Stephen responding to some comment I made about the evening, blurted out: "He is a better preacher than you, Dad". At that moment, I lost control of the car on the icy road and it virtually rotated 180 degrees until I was facing the opposite direction and the boys started screaming. Back came my response "That will teach you my boy for saying that!".

Jean on Prime TV - Four became Five

On April 14th 1980 Andrew was born. We were anticipating the birth with great joy, wondering whether this would be a gift of a girl. That was not to be, the words ringing in Jean's ear from the midwife was: 'It's a boy, Mrs Rees'. That was not a disappointment, we were thankful for a safe delivery and a healthy baby. And the story from this point has been one of profound thankfulness for the blessing and joy that Andrew has been to us.

I mustn't get ahead of myself. Jean was aware that she was about to give birth in the early evening of the 13th April. We arranged for our friend Marjorie Bateman to come and stay with the children and I took Jean in to the maternity ward at University Hospital. Early in the morning on the 14th, Andrew was born and this for me was the first time I had been at the birth of any one of our sons. It was awesome and wonderful – the miracle of birth and new life was beautiful.

It turned out that at this particular date, there was a significant rise in the number of births. It apparently was all connected to the miner's strike, for nine months earlier the government had to ration the supply of electricity and the area was under a blackout. Strange connection between blackout and births, but I guess you can work that puzzle out.

April 14th, 1980, UOW Hospital
New arrival – Andrew David Rees

This was an event that the press homed in on. They paid a visit to the maternity ward and there it was, broadcasted on BBC Wales news, an older Mum, Jean Rees, looking wonderful, holding her beautiful baby in her lap.

Welcome Home Mum and
Andrew [1980]

When I took the boys, later that afternoon to see their new brother who was in a ward of cots with all the new arrivals, Paul's comment was: "Andrew looks so beautiful, all the others look like rabbits!" Jean came home a few days later to be royally welcomed by us, with the boys having covered the garage door with a welcome home message. Some of Paul's contemporaries in the area made fun of the welcome home banner, but this didn't diminish the joy of the occasion.

Merciful Deliverance

In 1983, during our summer vacation, we were on our way for a holiday in Herne Bay, Kent. We had booked up at a Christian hotel and the guest speaker was Brian Edwards. We were travelling out of London on the M2. Jean was driving, doing around 60 miles an hour and I was enjoying listening to cricket, England were playing the Australians and Botham was batting. It was midday. I was absorbed and contented. Then Jean spoke: "I cannot control the steering wheel". At that moment time froze. I grasped the steering wheel, only to find that by then it was vibrating furiously and I couldn't hold it. The car veered to the left, crossing over from the fast lane, through the second and first lane, before hitting a barrier which it rolled over. It was all in slow motion, the car ended up buried in trees, but thankfully the right way up. My immediate concern was the safety of the family.

The three children were sitting in the back, with Andrew in a child safety seat in the middle. Stephen had held on to Andrew to keep him safe. At that point I was overwhelmed with fear, because I thought the car could burst into flames, so I wanted to get everyone out of the car quickly. It was with great difficulty that I opened the door and we all eventually got out safely. Yes, we were fearful and disorientated and in a state of shock. The car was written off. Paul's main concern was whether his guitar had been damaged! When the police arrived, we discovered that a man had been killed at that precise point a week earlier. He had hit the same barrier but his car had been pushed back towards other traffic. The previous accident had bent the barrier, which in our case was a real mercy as it allowed our car to roll over it, rather than be pushed back towards other traffic.

Herne Bay Holiday, Trip to France – 1983
Paul; Jean, Paul, Mervyn Burnell; Jean, Andrew; Stuart & Marjorie Bateman, Stephen

Another great blessing was that people from Cardiff [Burnell's, Bateman's] who were staying at the same hotel, turned up about 30 minutes after the accident and took care of us. This incident speaks of God's preserving mercy of our lives. He had a purpose for each one of us, and I trust that the unfolding narrative of these memoirs, underlines this reality. It is worth noting, that Brian Edwards in his morning mediations spoke of God's sovereignty in life, history and salvation and that proved significant in Paul's own theological development.

Making News - an unenviable Soccer performance

None of the boys were particularly sporty, although Andrew played for Rhiwbina Junior Football team. There was one memorable game. It was a Saturday morning and they were playing against a gifted Ely team. Ely won by ten goals to none, which was a devastating defeat. The reality was that the Rhiwbina team could not match the robust, physical game of Ely. They were too timid, too gentle and less confrontational. The game was given publicity by the local paper 'South Wales Echo' and Rhiwbina were described as 'no-hopers', as they had not won one single match all season. You would imagine that after that Andrew would have given up, but he loved playing too much for that. Once he transitioned to Secondary School, there was the opportunity to play in another team, with older boys but unfortunately the matches were on a Sunday, and so that was the end of his football career!

High School: Fire and Head Boy

Both Paul and Stephen proceeded from Rhiwbina Junior School to Llanishan High School, to study for their GCSE's and A Levels. The catchment School was Whitchurch High School, but we made the choice of Llanishan because of the number Christian teachers that we knew who taught there. Some were members of Bethesda. Andrew on the other hand went on to Whitchurch.

Both Paul, Stephen and Andrew progressed from High School to study at University. Paul majored on the Sciences and went to the University of London to study dentistry. Stephen followed the Arts to study at the University of Exeter, majoring on English, Drama and Education. Andrew, pursued the Sciences and went to Exeter University to study Computer Science. They all graduated with their respective Honours degrees. I will pick up in another chapter how their careers have developed.

High School in the main went without any great incidences, except for one occasion with Paul. The Head of Student Welfare, Mrs Down, who was a member of Bethesda, rang up to tell us that Paul through his actions could have burnt the School down! We wondered whether he had picked up any tips from our neighbour and MP, Gwilym Jones. The case against Paul was that he had been playing around with a magnifying glass, trying to light some grass. From what I recall of growing up, that was some innocent fun. This was not fun for Mrs Down, so we apologised and said that we would speak to him about it.

Stephen received the accolade of being elected head boy. He is particularly relational, charming and the girls found him attractive.

Reaching Milestones

Celebrated Jean's 70th birthday, at an hotel in Wotton-Under-Edge, Tortworth in Nov. 2012, and my 70th in a house we rented in Llandudno in April, 2013. These celebrations are captured in two Apple photographic albums.

Celebrated our Golden wedding anniversary in 2015. Rented a house to accommodate all of us in Bronygarth, Oswestry.

The University of Glamorgan

During this period the Polytechnic had received its Charter to become the University of Glamorgan in 1992. Its evolution from

College of Technology [1958], through its Polytechnic designation [1970] to University status brought many challenges. It was the catalyst to significant advances; in a range of courses from under-graduate to post-graduate, number of Departments, establishment of Faculties and number of students. At the time of retirement in 2010, there were over 20,000 students, some of these were from overseas franchises. This meant that over the years I have had to surf many initiatives; work hard to maintain excellence and academic credibility in a savagely competitive academic world.

I submitted my research thesis in 1976 and following a viva was awarded my PhD based on the work entitled 'Digital Processing of System Responses', I was admitted a Fellow of the Institution of Electrical Engineers on the 6th July, 1988. I was promoted to Principal Lecturer in 1979, Deputy Head [1987], Reader and Associate Head [1991] and Associate Head/Director of Research [2003].

This also meant serving on various University Committees, like Academic Board, Faculty Board, Quality Standard Committee and serving on validation events both at the University and at other Institutions.

David explaining to a government minister an expert system research project. [1980]

An initiative that I was greatly involved with was the Teaching Company Scheme. This scheme was set up by the government to bring Universities and Industry together in the training of graduates, which also facilitated the transfer of skills in both directions, from University to Industry and vice-versa. One scheme that I managed, for a period of 11 years was with STC Cable manufacturing based in Newport. The main activity of the work was related to the manufacturing and design process for fibre-optic cable. Around 10 graduates came through this scheme and many of them went on to have very successful careers in Industry. A number of them registered their projects for a Master's degree, and a number of scientific publications ensued, published in the International Wire and Cable Symposium and 'Expert Systems' conferences. The expert system work used in the design of fibre-optic cables, proved very timely and was shortlisted for an UK Design Council award[14]. My teaching company associate on this project was Llyr Roberts, who came from Llandeilo. His father was the chief executive of the Urdd Eisteddfod.

In terms of using my control engineering expertise I was involved with lecturing at an IEE summer school at Balliol College, Oxford on 'Industrial Digital Control Systems' [1985-89]. I was joint editor of a book published by the IEE in their Control Engineering Series, based on this material. For further details refer to Appendix IV. It is a continuing surprise to me, that I still get, thirty years later some royalties [small!] from the sale of the book.

I served on numerous IEE Committees, including being the Chairman of the IEE Control Applications Professional group and a member of the IEE Computing and Control Division. I was also a HEFCE Specialist assessor for both Mechanical Engineering (1994/95) and Electrical and Electronic Engineering (1995/96) and a referee for the IEE Proceedings: Control Theory and Applications and also other learned journals (IEEE/ECJ etc).

I will in another section cover the opportunities brought about through my University career.

Members of my Research Unit
[60th birthday, 2003].

During this period, I was field leader of the Electro-Mechanical field, which covered 46 modules and eight members of staff. I also was the head of the research unit in system identification and control, which I built up over the years to be a successful research unit. Pro. Guoping Liu, took over the leadership of the group [next person to my right], when I approached retirement.

Once the children were old enough Jean had two stints working part-time at the University of Cardiff. She worked firstly in the Department of Zoology for Prof. Bellamy, and then secondly was the PA for Prof. Phil Cook in the Town and Reginal Planning Department. The two stints were separated by the birth of our third son, Andrew. She retired when she reached the age of sixty.

14

LIVING STONES

The reader by now must realise that church is important to me and my family. That was the primary reason for our move from Ponypridd to Cardiff.

The metaphors in the New Testament for the church are varied and powerful; the body of Christ, Bride of Christ, family of God, God's house and Temple of God. In this last metaphor Christian believers are living stones, making up the Temple of God, with Christ as the foundation and cornerstone and the Holy Spirit indwelling it. [1 Cor. 3:11,16-17; Eph. 2:19-22; 1 Peter 2:5-7]. These are metaphors that embrace the church universal but also find expression in the local church. It is a wonderful privilege to be part of God's universal church and to see that expressed in the membership of a local church. A church by its very definition, should be committed to the Apostolic teaching and therefore proclaims the gospel and seeks the honour of the Lord Jesus Christ. Belonging to a local church means that it is a dynamic, vibrant fellowship bringing together people, from different backgrounds, ethnicity and education who are united under the Lordship of Christ. They are 'Living Stones' making up the habitation of God by his Spirit and the title of this section seeks to emphasise that.

Bethesda in Rhiwbina is an independent evangelical church whose roots are in the open brethren tradition.[15,16,17] At the time we joined it had a membership of around 110 and was seen as a good Bible teaching church, well balanced and which had avoided some of the extremes that can exist within the Brethren tradition.

What was particularly appealing was its children and young people's work. We thought it was important to have a clear biblical input into the spiritual development of the children and for us as a family. We are thankful to God, as we look back on those years, the way we were blessed as a family. As the children became teenagers this became even more important. All three sons came to a personal faith in Christ when they were children. The young people's work was led at that time by David Colman, who was a gifted leader. Here is an extract from a recent email sent by Paul to David, reflection on this period:

"Your leadership of the Young People's Sunday evening meetings created a community where there was a buzz about singing God's praises and learning from the bible.

Those creative weeks where we studied bible sections like the Sermon on the Mount, James etc and got people to write sketches and songs and then show their work was so much fun.

I also see how you managed to convince young people to come out to a mid-week prayer meeting by the prospect of returning to your home for some good banter as well as some good Q&A discussions. The prayer times could be a bit dull - but the after hospitality kept pulling us out!"

In 1980, just before Andrew was born, I was invited to serve as an elder, which I did for 34 years. The latter part of that period, seventeen years of it, I served as the secretary and chairman of the elders. When I joined the eldership, we were 9 elders, but over time this reduced to six. My great soul mate and mentor, was Dr Ivor Strode, who also lectured at the University of Glamorgan. I had the privilege of taking his funeral in 2017.

To serve as an elder was a great privilege and I was wonderfully supported by my wife, Jean, who provided the hospitality for visiting preachers and missionaries. This was no mean task, particularly with bringing up a family at the same time. Serving in this way was rewarding but often challenging as one sought to 'shepherd the flock of God'. A number of initiatives were introduced to provide a greater structure to the teaching ministry within the church, and often these were initially resisted but over time became accepted as the norm, and I would like to think was a blessing to the church.

G. Watkins, M Horlock,
I Strode, D Rees [All Elders] [1998]

The church' tradition in the main was to use the teaching gift within the membership, as well as invited lay preachers. There were a number of gifted men in the church at that time, to name just a few, of the older generation, Ivor Strode, Malcolm Horlock, Mervyn Jones, Graham Watkins and David Colman. They were men who gave themselves to the study of the Bible. In more recent years some able young men have emerged, like, John Bodger, Stuart Scammell and Mark Bodger.

I also made my regular contribution to the teaching programme and was involved with preaching in different churches, mainly of

Brethren persuasion. When Paul and Stephen were teenagers, I led the young people's class, which was run on a Sunday afternoon. This I took over from Dr Strode.

My final bequest to the church, which I was the prime champion for, was the employment of a full-time worker, to work in the community and provide an input to the teaching programme. We employed Dr Jonathan Newell, who had served as a missionary in Malawi, an able teacher and a passionate evangelist. Unfortunately, after we left Cardiff circumstances changed; things began to unravel and Jonathan decided to move on.

Anyone involved with pastoral ministry knows that it can be challenging. People, even the Lord's people are different, varied and sometimes difficult. Sin is a universal problem and all of us have been scarred by it. We are not insulated from the changes in the culture around and consequently that can and often does invade the believing community with the result that marriages are in trouble, business partners are at loggerheads and believing children become rebellious. Even relationships between co-workers on the mission field can become fractious to the point of alienating. In addition to that we are caught up in a broken world, where sorrow and suffering is woven into the fabric of people's lives. All of this became part of our ministry as elders and we had to seek the Lord's wisdom to know how to resolve them, as best as we could, to His glory. This was often demanding, particularly with a busy full-time job as well.

The unique meeting for independent churches like Bethesda, was the 'breaking of bread' service. This was and for some churches, even now, is one of their distinctives. This service would been seen as fulfilling the Lord's command: "Do this in remembrance of me" [1 Cor. 11:24] and it would be weekly, because that is what the early church did [Acts 20:7; 1 Cor. 16:1].

The whole of the service would be devoted to open-worship, where different male members would lead the congregation in praise. The overarching focus would be on the life, death, resurrection and enthronement of the Lord Jesus. A theme would be introduced at the start of the service, by for example a choice of hymn or a reading of the scripture, and often that theme would continue throughout the service. If the Bible was read and commented on, then the expectation would be that it seamlessly contributed to the worship theme of the service. This particular structure a younger generation found somewhat inhibiting, but for the older Christian who was immersed in the scriptures and in this tradition, they found it profoundly moving and spiritual. The greater ability you had of engaging with and progressing the theme, the more you were seen as being led by the Holy Spirit.

Out of this view of the Lord's supper emerged a whole genre of hymnology, which is rich in its Christology. Here are three examples:

Amidst us our Beloved stands, And bids us view His pierced hands, Points to his wounded feet and side – Blest emblems of the Crucified.

Or:

No bone of Thee was broken, Thou spotless paschal Lamb! Of life and peace a token, To us who know Thy name; The Head, for all the members, The curse, the vengeance bore, And God, our God, remembers, His people's sins no more.

Or:

Lamb of God! Our souls adore Thee, While upon Thy face we gaze; There the Father's love and glory, Shine in all their brightest rays; Thine almighty power and wisdom, All creation's works proclaim; Heaven and earth alike confess Thee, As the ever great "I AM."

This was spiritually enriching and invigorating. It often gave a foretaste of heaven but sometimes it could disappoint, because it relied upon spiritual discernment and the willingness of brethren to submit to one another and be tuned in to the work of the Spirit. That did not always happen and sometimes contributions were less than profitable. Those less 'spiritually tuned' could misuse this liberty.

There are some humorous memories.

Memory 1: One was the prayer of Trevor Studley, a bachelor who lived with his sister. He worked with the forestry commission in

Carmarthenshire and he very kindly gave us a wedding gift. He loved to quote the third verse of the hymn 'Lead, kindly Light, amid th' encircling gloom', which reads:

"So long Thy pow'r has blest me, sure it still
Wilt lead me on,
O'er moor and fen, o'er crag and torrent, till
The night is gone,
And with the morn those angel faces smile,
Which I have loved long since, and lost awhile"

Mervyn Jones, who has an acute sense of humour, commented, "Trevor, with his moor and fen, o'er crag and torrent, has come down Heol-y-bont, Pant-bach Rd and Lon-Penllyn again this morning!"

Memory 2: Another was the contributions of Mr Trevor Dowen. He would stand up from where he was sitting, never go up to the pulpit, and proceed to read and speak, and invariably it was enigmatic. One recollection were the words: "Movement is deceptive – if I were sitting in a train and another train were leaving another platform; it would appear as if I were moving. Movement is deceptive! To this day, I don't know what point he was making, at least something registered with me!

Memory 3: One Sunday morning, we had a visitor from Llangeler, West Wales. His brother married Jean's aunt, Martha Perkins from Maesybont. Mr Jones, exercised his liberty and took part in public worship, but his prayer was in Welsh. The next Sunday morning, Mr Hussey took to the pulpit and proceeded to exhort the church that what had happened the previous Sunday was not according to scripture, because there was no one to interpret the prayer. He had missed the obvious point, he had not spoken in tongues, we were in Cardiff, the capital city of Wales, Welsh is the national language and if there had been the necessity then a number of us could have provided a translation. Mr Hussey was a stickler for 'assembly order' but this time he had overstepped the mark.

The fellowship was very active evangelistically, running holiday Bible clubs, Bible exhibitions, evangelistic events and Christianity explored courses and over the years we saw people coming through to faith in Christ. They were never in great numbers but we did receive encouragements.

We had the opportunity to run a number of courses in our home, where a number of my post-graduate students attended. They were mainly from China, but not exclusively so, some from India, Cyprus and Germany.

Christianity Explored Group
[2006] – Christmas

For a number of years, the church organised a church weekend away with a guest speaker giving four messages across the weekend. These were always enjoyable, spiritually stimulating and beneficial to the life of the church.

Church Weekend at Brunel Manor, October, 1995. Guest Preacher, Paul Young, who gave four messages on the Sermon on the Mount.

One of the great blessings of this period at Bethesda, was the number of young people that went into full-time Christian ministry – Robert Lacy [now deceased - Cardiff], Alan John [Pastor of an Independent Church in Swansea], Stuart Phillips [Associate Minister at St John's Dukinfield, Manchester], Mark Reed [Baptist minister], Naomi Hill [COE Women's ministry], Eunice Jones [Pakistan], Rosemary Atkinson [deceased – Austria], Christopher Williams [Pastor, Lisvane Baptist] and my three sons, Paul [Pastor, Charlotte Chapel, Edinburgh], Stephen [Vicar, All Saints, Crowborough] and Andrew [Pastor, Surrey Chapel, Norwich]. In my view there were two primary influences that were formative in the development of these young people. Firstly, the gospel ethos of the church and secondly, the leadership in the young people's ministry.

15

ARROWS IN MY QUIVER

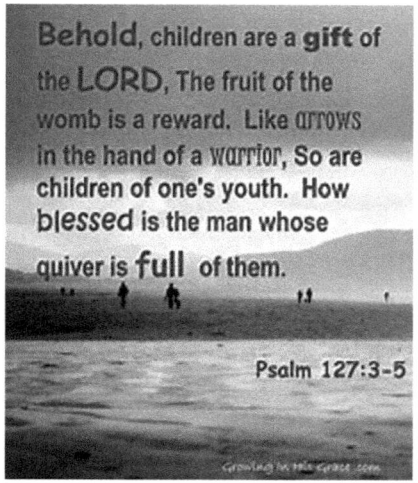

Behold, children are a **gift** of the LORD, The fruit of the womb is a reward. Like arrows in the hand of a warrior, So are children of one's youth. How blessed is the man whose quiver is full of them.

Psalm 127:3-5

As I come to write this section, I am constrained to reflect on the words of the Psalmist 'Blessed is the man whose quiver is full of them'. The sense of God's blessing and faithfulness, which both Jean and I profoundly feel, as we think of the three sons born to us, Paul, Stephen and Andrew, and then their subsequent marriages to Shiona, Jenny and Grace respectively. Then the joy of having offspring from those marriages; to Paul and Shiona, Nathan, Amy, Bethany, Tom; to Stephen and Jenny, Zachary, Daisy, Molly, Rosie and Winnie; to Andrew and Grace, Tilly, Betsy and Vivi. That is a remarkable 'quiver full'!

Paul Lewis Rees

Paul as we have already seen was born in Welwyn Garden City on the 9th May, 1968. He studied Dentistry at London Hospital and qualified in June 1990. He was very active in the Christian Union and became its President in 1988.

During his time in London, he attended, St Helen's, Bishopsgate and the rector at that time was Dick Lucas[18], who had a significant impact on his life and future ministry.

Paul with Dick Lucas [2008]

It was at this time he met Shiona MacDonald, at an UCCF conference in Oswestry. She was vice-president of the Christian Union at Glasgow University. After graduating he moved up to Dundee to practice dentistry but also to be closer to the woman in his life.

Paul and Shiona - March 21st, 1992

They got married at Greenview Evangelical church on Saturday, March 21st, 1992 and made their home in Glasgow. She is a wonderful help-meet for Paul. Paul went to work in a Glasgow dental practice. At this time, Paul became exercised about equipping himself for Christian ministry and so started the Cornhill one-year training course in 1993. This is run under the auspices of St Helen's, Bishopsgate. This meant a move for the young couple to London.

After completing the course, they returned to Scotland, with Paul more fully persuaded that his future was not in dentistry but in Christian ministry. Their first son, Nathan Zachary was born on 1st December, 1995 and in January, 1997 they moved to Sydney, Australia for Paul to study theology at Moore Bible College, an evangelical Anglican institution. He graduated three years later with an upper-second class Honours degree.

During his time in Australia, he served the first two years as a 'catechist' at St Thomas Anglican church and then for the final year, joined the Department of Evangelism of the Sydney diocese being trained under the leadership of a great evangelist, John Charles Chapman, known as 'Chappo'.[19]

Department of Evangelism, Sydney
[Chappo – last on the right] [1999]

During this time in Australia, their family grew, Amy Jean was born on December 20, 1997 and Bethany Anne born on the 17th August, 1999. They returned to the UK in 2000 and Paul was appointed as Assistant Pastor at Highfield Free Church in Cardiff in August, 2000 of that year. Their return to Cardiff was however, somewhat short lived, as in January, 2002 Paul was called to be the Senior Pastor at Christ the Redeemer Church in Spokane.

They moved to America in January, 2002 and were there until July, 2009, when they returned to the UK. Thomas Lewis was born in Spokane on 30th Nov. 2002.

Christ the Redeemer Church [was Grace Baptist]

They were blessed in their ministry and saw the merger between Christ The Redeemer Church and Grace Baptist Church in Jan. 2005. A new opportunity for ministry commenced in 2005 with a weekly radio Bible teaching programme called 'Preach the Word', broadcasted by Moody Bible Radio.

On returning to the UK, Paul was appointed Senior Pastor of Charlotte Chapel, Edinburgh. He was inducted as Pastor on 12th September, 2009 and he has continued in that role up to now.

During this time at the Chapel he has overseen the move to a new building, from Rose Street, to Shandwick Place. This is an old Church of Scotland building, which they moved into in 2016. The church is a vibrant witness to the gospel at the very heart of Edinburgh.

Charlotte Chapel, Shandwick Place, Edinburgh.

Scottish Rees family. [2019]

Thomas, Bethany, Nathan, Paul, Shiona, Amy

Stephen Philip Rees

Stephen was born in Luton on the 13th January, 1970. At the age of 18, he went to study, English, Drama and Education at Exeter University and graduated with an upper second Honours degree in 1992. During this time, through a church home group he met Jenny Burrowes, a committed Christian from Cockfosters. They jelled, fell in love, shared a passion to follow the Lord Jesus and in due time got engaged and then married.

123

Stephen and Jenny – 30th July, 1994

They married at Christchurch, Cockfosters on Saturday, 30th July in 1994. The ceremony was conducted by a delightful Welsh vicar, Tony Rees, who gave great support and advice to them as they pursued options for ministry.

Stephen after graduating returned to Cardiff for a teaching post at 'Bryn Hafod' primary school, Llanrumney.

Following his marriage, he moved to Whetstone, London and had a teaching job at 'St Mary Magdalene' primary school. On the 6 May, 1996, they had their first child, Zachary Dafydd John.

Options for ministry opened up for Stephen and he decided in the first instance to do the one year, Cornhill course full-time in 1996/97.

Following this he became an assistant pastor at Enfield Free Evangelical church on the 6th Sept., 1998. This opening followed on the recommendation of David Jackman, who was heading the Cornhill Trust at that time. His commendation is worth repeating:

"Stephen is thoroughly committed to Scripture, in its authority and inerrancy, and to the preaching and teaching of the Word as the means by which men and women are won to Christ and built up in Him. Stephen works hard at his preparation and is committed to expository preaching. He has a great gift of presenting truth in an attractive, contemporary and relevant way, without in any way compromising the force of the message. Because his own life is very much under the authority of the Lord through the Word, he can be trusted to preach it accurately and with great faithfulness......."

On 19 May, 1998, they had their first daughter, Daisy Zipporah. After a couple of years, Stephen decided that he would benefit from further theological training, so he resigned from his post at Enfield Free, and went to do a three-year degree course in theology at Oak Hill Theological College, an Anglican Evangelical College in Southgate.

Stephen, Theological Student at Oak Hill [2001]

He started his course in September 2000 and graduated in the Summer of 2003 with an Honours degree in Theological and Pastoral Studies. During this period at College, Molly-Mary Jemima was born, on the 8th March, 2000. Probably the most significant decision in terms of the future direction of his Christian ministry was made at this time when he became an Anglican ordinand. They had the gift of another daughter on the 14th June, 2002, when Rosie-Tellula Hannah was born. Stephen graduated in June, 2003 and was ordained on 29th June at the Cathedral Church of St. Peter, Gloucester.

After graduating they moved to Moreton-In-Marsh, when Stephen became the curate at St. David's. He served with Rev'd Stephen Wookey, an evangelical vicar, who had spent some of his earlier years at All Souls, Langham Place. London.

After three years, he became the Vicar of Christchurch, Little Heath on September 12th, 2006. This was a significant period in Stephen's ministry as he saw the Church grow and become evangelically more robust.

Stephen being poster-boy in the Oak Hill College Prospectus. [2008]

During this period Christchurch had its first curate and numerous placement students. It was in 2013, they had the wonderful gift of an adopted daughter, Winnie Florence Martha, born on Feb. 2nd, 2011.

All Saints Crowborough

In 2016, Stephen and the family moved to Crowborough, East Sussex, when he became the Vicar of All Saints Church. He was licensed on February 26th. This is a significant church in the diocese, numerically very strong and has established a reputation for faithful Biblical expository preaching. It has had a heritage of evangelical ministers.

Crowborough Rees family

Left to right: Rosie, Molly, Winnie, Jenny, Stephen, Daisy, Zachary, Alfie [husband of Daisy]

[2019]

Andrew David Rees

Andrew was born on April 14th, 1980. He is the only Rees boy, born in Wales. He went to Exeter University in 1998 to study Computer Science. He was active in the Christian Union, and made St Leonard's Church his spiritual home.

'Men of the future' at the Royal Albert Hall. EN article 2003. Andrew with Peter Sanlon

This was a London Men's Convention event organised by Cornhill Trust.

Andrew with Aneirin Glyn
[2019]

There were two people at St Leonard's who were influential in Andrew's Christian development. One was Aneirin Glyn, the student worker and the other was the curate Alasdair Paine, who is now the Senior Minister of the Church of Great St Andrew's, Cambridge. Aneirin has strong Welsh connections, his grandfather (Henry Rees) came from Llanelli and was a missionary for many years in India. He is now the church leader at St. Benet, the Metropolitan Welsh Church situated at Blackfriars, also leads the Sunday afternoon congregation at St. Helens, Bishopsgate.

After graduating, Andrew joined St Ebbes, Oxford in 2001 as a ministry apprentice working primarily amongst students. At the same time, Aneirin returned to Oxford University where he had graduated from to do his PhD in Mathematics, so their friendship continued.

After two years at St Ebbes, Andrew did a teacher's training course at Kings College, London University and this was followed by a teaching post at Sutton Grammar School [2004]. He remained in teaching for three years, gaining promotion to be head of the computer science discipline in the meantime. He however, felt that his future was in full-time Christian ministry and in 2007 joined the staff of St Helens Bishopsgate as a student worker.

He remained at St Helens for two years and then decided to do an honour's degree at Oak Hill Theological College. This he commenced in 2010.

During his time at St Helens, he met a delightful young lady, Grace Garnham from Newcastle who was working in the church. This was the beginning of a love match that culminated in marriage on the 18th July, 2009 at Christchurch, Little Heath.

While studying at Oak Hill, Andrew did one year as a trainee minister with Spicer Street Evangelical Church in St Albans and the next two years at St Paul's in Hadley Wood. The latter appointment provided for them a spacious vicarage, which proved a great blessing.

Andrew and Grace Wedding Day - 18th July, 2009

On 2012, two became three with the birth of Matilda Mai on January 4th.

He graduated in June, 2013 with an upper second-class Honours degree in Theological and Pastoral Studies.

He was inducted as an Assistant Pastor at Woodgreen, Evangelical Church, Worcester on the 15th September, 2013 and became an Associate Pastor on 4th Sept. 2016.

Woodgreen Evangelical Church Worcester

The time in Worcester proved very encouraging and it was spiritually fruitful. They were very happy days with long-term friendships established. It was also a time for the family to grow, when they had two beautiful additions. On July 25th, 2014 Betsy Renée was born, and on Oct 7th, 2016, Viviana Lucille arrived. All wonderful gifts from a gracious and sovereign creator.

In May, 2019, Andrew and family moved to Norwich, to take on the role of Lead Pastor at Surrey Chapel, an FIEC church. Surrey Chapel is a modern, busy church, but it traces its roots back over 150 years in Norwich. It has a strong heritage of preaching within the evangelical tradition.

Norwich Rees family – Andrew, Vivi, Tilly, Grace, Betsy [2019]

The Rees Clan

Christmas 2018 – Crowborough

David, Jean, Daisy, Jenny, Betsy, Molly, Bethany, Tilly, Nathan, Winnie, Amy, Stephen, Rosie, Grace, Vivi, Andrew, Shiona, Zachary, Tom, Paul.

16

WINDOWS ON THE WORLD

With academic life, there comes the opportunity for travel. Science is a universal language and the pursuit of its advancement crosses over international borders. Every discipline has its national and international institutions, which are set up to maintain excellence in that specific area and provide a forum where ideas are explored and progress reported.

**David with Ceri Evans –
Awarded his PhD in 1998[20].
IEEE conference - Ottawa, 1997**

These events can have grand titles like 'World Congress', or 'International Conference', others a more low key descriptor, like a 'Colloquium on..' or a 'Workshop on..'. However, the organisers of such events are invariably learned Institutions, facilitated by University research groups. The Institutions have their Journals and Conferences to report on the most recent developments.

My subject area and research activity have straddled a range of engineering disciplines, so you can see from my publications which are given in Appendix IV, that the work has found its outlet in IEE, IEEE, IFAC, ASME, IERE, ACC, UKSC, EUREL, IWCS

Journals or conferences. All work published are peer reviewed, the conferences less rigorously so, compared to Journal publications.

October 8th, 1996 David receiving from Prof. M G Rodd the 'F C Williams Premium' at IEE, Computing and Control Divisional Board dinner, Savoy Place, London

One of the accolades achieved by my research group was winning in 1996 the IEE 'FC Williams Premium', for the paper entitled "Identifying linear models of systems suffering non-linear distortions with gas turbine application", which was a Journal paper jointly authored by myself and two of my colleagues. [Refer to the publications listed in the appendix for the full reference.] The credit for this award should in fact go to a very able PhD student I had, Ceri Evans.

Sadly, some years later he took his own life, ostensibly because of difficulties in his relationship with his partner, who became the leader of 'Plaid Cymru' in the Welsh Assembly.

Later, in my academic career I had the opportunity of taking Jean with me to some of these international conferences. That clearly was a great privilege and it enabled us together to have these 'windows on the world'. We have travelled widely, either through my work, or the cruising we have done in the past 15 years. Appendix V gives an overview of my/our overseas travel. Clearly, there is a lot of material to draw upon, many windows which we can look through that would give us a multifaceted and a wide spectrum view of the world. I plan to limit my horizon, and so I propose to structure this section around a coherent theme which I loosely relate to a Christian perspective.

1986/87/88/89 Oxford - IEE Summer School at Balliol College on Industrial Digital Control Systems.

In Oxford's St Giles there is a huge Victorian memorial to the Oxford Martyrs, close to the spot where they were burned at the stake - Nicholas Ridley and Hugh Latimer, in 1555. The third, Thomas Cranmer, was burnt five months later on 21 March 21, 1556.

Lord Jesus, receive my spirit . . . I see the heavens open and Jesus standing at the right hand of God. [Cranmer]

Play the man, Master Ridley; we shall this day light such a candle, by God's grace in England, as I trust shall never be put out. [Latimer]

1988 Avignon - Workshop on Expert Systems

Known as the City of the Popes. Between 1309 and 1377, during the Avignon Papacy, seven successive popes resided here. Papal control persisted until 1791 when everything changed with the French revolution.

135

1989 Atlanta, Georgia IWCS Conference

Birth home of Dr Martin Luther King and Ebenezer Baptist Church, Atlanta , 'which was his first pastored'

"*When evil men plot, good men must plan. When evil men burn and bomb, good men must build and bind. When evil men shout ugly words of hatred, good men must commit themselves to the glories of love. Where evil men would seek to perpetuate an unjust status quo, good men must seek to bring into being a real order of justice*" Martin Luther King

2001 Pretoria – Control Theory & Applications Conf.
Birth home of Nelson Mandela, Soweto

"*What counts in life is not the mere fact that we have lived. It is what difference we have made to the lives of others that will determine the significance of the life we lead*". Nelson Mandela

1989/1995/2008 Beijing - First visit was to give a paper at a Conference on System simulation and Scientific computing.

On my first visit I received a visit to my hotel room from a Chinese post-graduate student with the gift of a book on artificial intelligence. I reciprocated and gave him a gift of a Bible. His response was; "Did I write it?"!

This pic was taken on my third visit, 2008 when Jean came with me. Taken at Badaling.

2008 Seoul, South Korea – IFAC World Congress

Jean in Seoul. [2008]

This pic was taken on the South side of the military demarcation line established in 1953. The Korean Peninsula was divided along the 38th parallel north from 1945 until 1950.

The sculpture provides a powerful image of a divided people, which world leaders are doing their best to reconcile. The book of Ephesians, chapter 2 provides a window on how Christ through his death has brought together people who are alienated from each other.

2000 Cambridge – IEE UKACC - Control 2000

Over the main entrance of the Cavendish Laboratory, the home of the Department of Physics in the University of Cambridge, is an inscription: *'The works of the Lord are great; sought out of all them that have pleasure therein'*. This is in Latin.

It is in English, at the entrance of the new building.

2004 Boston-IEEE ACC

It is in Boston that D L Moody was converted, in a shoe shop on April 21st, 1855. He established a number of Christian ministries, including the Moody Institute, which in turn set up its aviation ministry.

This trains pilots for missionary work and is based in Spokane Valley. This pic was taken in 2007. Some of the training pilots were members of 'Christ the Redeemer' church and we were taken for a flight over the valley, including a flight over Paul's house. It was not an experience I greatly enjoyed!

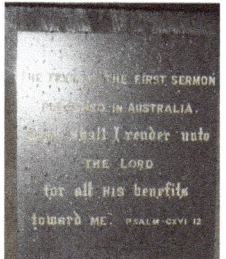

1998 Sydney, Australia The right-hand plaque reads: To the Glory of God and in Commemoration of the first Christian Service held in Australia, Feb. 3rd, 1788. Rev Richard Johnson B A The Chaplain being the Preacher.

2005 Portland, USA - IEEE ACC

We were staying at the Hilton – the carnival was passing and we watched it as it passed the Hotel. From the parade came a shout: '*An encounter with Jesus Christ is better than a night in the Hilton*". We responded with a loud Amen, which took him by surprise!

2003 Vail, Colorado. IEEE Instrumentation and Measurement Conference

 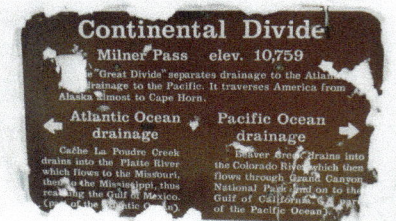

Leadville - a gold/silver mine which attracted a lot of speculators in 1860. Milner pass leads to the point where you meet the continental divide. Many diggers lost their lives in their pursuit of gold – reminded me of the words of the Psalmist, that God's word is *'more precious than gold, than much pure gold'* [Psa. 19:10]. Jean came with me and we flew on from here to Spokane.

2002 San Francisco IEEE conference - San Francisco Golden Bridge and Crater Lake

Travelled to Spokane via Lake Tahoe, Crater Lake and up the Oregon Coast. Crater Lake is the world' 6th deepest lake. Think of God's promise – Micah 7:19.

2007 Kos – ECC conference

Took a boat trip to Patmos to visit the cave of the Apocalypse, which is claimed as the place where John was exiled to. [Rev. 1:9]

This was a profoundly moving experience as the Greek Orthodox Church minister read in Greek, from Rev. 1:12-20 the verses that describe the vision of the Son of Man, that John received, and his response: *'When I saw him, I fell at his feet as though dead'*. It was a memorable occasion that resonated deeply with me.

1996/97/98 Athens – collaboration with CMA.

Also, visited with a cruise in 2018. Mars Hill looking over on to the Acropolis.

It is here that Paul preached, calling on the Athenians to repent because God has appointed a day when he will judge the world in righteousness through Jesus Christ. [Acts 17:30-31]

2018 Medina, Malta – P&O Cruise

Stone carving of Paul at the entrance to the old city, commemorating the occasion, when he was bitten by a viper and he shakes it off. [Acts 28: 1-6]

2018 Messina, Sicily - P& O Cruise

This is the cathedral and it has a remarkable clock. At midday, there was a ten-minute spectacular when the lion roared three times followed by the cock crowing three times, then the music of Annamaria. It reminded me of the Lion roaring in the book of Amos the prophet [Amos 3:4] and the cock crowing after the denial of Peter [Matt. 26:34,74].

2018 Heraklion, Crete - P&O Cruise

Visited the church of Titus. Titus was Paul's emissary to Crete, he left him there to strengthen the church and establish elders. He was bold enough to quote one of their prophets who described them as liars etc. [Titus 1:12]. He proclaimed to them, the kindness and love of God revealed in the Saviour, Jesus Christ. [Titus 3:4]

1998/2006 Minneapolis – ACC conference

In 2006, went on to Spokane, via Chicago and Wheaton. Visited the Billy Graham Museum at Wheaton. Provides interesting displays on the history of evangelism, highlights of Billy Graham's life and ministry, and is a graphic presentation of the gospel.

1997 Ottawa, Canada – IEEE Conference

Travelled via Toronto - visited Niagara Falls. This is a group of three water-falls, the largest of the three is Horseshoe Falls also known as Canadian Falls, which straddles the border between Canada and the USA.

The noise was awesome, reminded me of the words concerning the suffering of the Messiah in Psalm 42:7. *"Deep calls to deep in the roar of your waterfalls; all your waves and breakers have swept over me."*

2013 Jerusalem Organised Trip to Israel

This was a wonderful visit, profoundly moving as you visited the ancient sites: Golgotha, Garden Tomb, Gethsemane, Mount of Olives, the Gehenna Valley, the Old City of David, Pool of Siloam, Nehemiah's wall and gates etc.

A reminder that Christianity is rooted in authentic history.

1995 Geneva – Visit a Cable Company – TC collaboration with STC

Reformation Monument: Guillaume Farel - the first to preach the Reformation in Geneva. John Calvin - leader of the Reformation movement and spiritual father of Geneva. Theodore Beza - Calvin's successor, born in Vezelay (France) and known for emphasizing Calvin's doctrine of predestination. John Knox- Scottish preacher, friend of Calvin, and founder of Presbyterianism in Scotland

2019 St Petersburg P&O Baltic Cruise

The Church of the Saviour on Spilled Blood is one of the main sights of Saint Petersburg, Russia.

Other names include the Church on Spilled Blood and the Cathedral of the Resurrection of Christ. Erected on the site, where political nihilists fatally wounded Emperor Alexander II, in March 1881. The church was constructed between 1883 and 1907.

2018 St Kitts, Caribbean, P&O Cruise

Lighthouse Baptist Church, Sandy Point - set up a monument to John Newton, whose connections with the island was as a slave trader. By God's grace, his life was turned round and he became a Christian and an abolitionist. Known best for his hymn:

Amazing Grace! How sweet the sound
That saved a wretch like me!
I once was lost, but now am found
Was blind, but now I see.

'Twas Grace that taught my heart to fear,
And Grace my fears relieved.
How precious did that Grace appear
The hour I first believed.

1990 Florida

Holiday - Silver Wedding Celebrations

Kennedy Space Centre

"The Earth reminded us of a Christmas tree ornament hanging in the blackness of space. As we got farther and farther away it diminished in size. Finally, it shrank to the size of a marble, the most beautiful marble you can imagine. That beautiful, warm, living object looked so fragile, so delicate, that if you touched it with a finger it would crumble and fall apart. Seeing this has to change a man, has to make a man appreciate the creation of God and the love of God." James Irwin

[He served as Apollo Lunar Module pilot for Apollo 15, the fourth human lunar landing. He was the eighth person to walk on the moon.]

2007 Yellowstone National Park

Went with Paul and family.

Old Faithful Geyser, spouting water high into the atmosphere. Old Faithful erupts every 35 to 120 minutes for 1.5 to 5 minutes. Its maximum height ranges from 90 to 184 feet. It is not the biggest or the most regular geyser in Yellowstone but it is the biggest regular geyser.

A spectacular sight to behold. Reminded of the words of Psalm 139:14 *"your works are wonderful; I know that full well"*

2009 St Louis, USA – ACC Conference

This is a memorial called 'Gateway to the West', which is along the Mississippi River. **The river** played an essential role in establishing St. Louis's identity as the gateway to the west. Early pioneers to open up the West were Lewis and Clark.

This reminds me of the voice calling in the wilderness *"Prepare the way of the Lord, make straight in the desert a highway for our God.... the glory of the Lord will be revealed..."* [Isa. 40:3-5]

2004 Boston – IEEE Conference

After the conference we toured Vermont, Maine, New Hampshire.

Visited Mount Washington Summit. It was spectacular – reminded of the words of Moses: *'Before the mountains were born or you brought forth the whole world, from everlasting to everlasting you are God'.* [Psa. 90:2]

17

EDINBURGH BECKONS

Providence has both its sunshine and its shadows, its beautifully unsullied blues skies and its clouds and storms. The Christian mind is one informed by God's mercy and one that calls us to trust whatever form that providence takes. We were about to discover what that meant when trials come.

It was sudden and unexpected. We had travelled up to Worcester to pick up Jean's car from our son Andrew. We returned to Cardiff on the same day, I was driving my own car, Jean was driving hers. Then the realisation that Jean was not functioning properly, she was not well, she was confused. It was something that I had slowly become aware of, but this particular day highlighted that there were issues that needed to be addressed. This was the start of a long emotional journey, which climaxed in the decision to move to be closer to one of our children.

The immediate decision was to have a doctor's appointment. This was early February, 2015. This resulted in the diagnosis of an over active thyroid which needed to be treated as a matter of urgency. To accelerate the process, we made the decision to go privately, with a Bristol Endocrine partnership. Given the diagnosis the thyroxin level in the body had to be stabilised through medication and only when this had been achieved, they would operate. This process of stabilisation seemed endless.

At this point we made the decision that the time had come for us to leave Cardiff and move to be closer to one of our children. We felt that it was important not to leave this decision too late, certainly before, *"the sun and the light and the moon and the stars grow dark, and the keepers of the house tremble"* using the metaphors of Ecclesiastes 12. The decision as to where we should move too was relatively easy as both Stephen and Andrew at that time were likely to move, but not sure where. Therefore, we decided on moving to Edinburgh and we put our house up for sale in May and we left the outcome in the Lord's hands.

During this time Jean's energy levels were diminishing and more worryingly, her eyesight was deteriorating. This prompted a visit to Specsavers on Nov. 27th, 2015, which resulted in a rapid referral to the Ophthalmic Department of the University of Wales Hospital and thyroxin eye disease was diagnosed. It turned out that both eyes had been affected which resulted in two orbital decompression operations, one on 17th December, 2015 and the other on the 21st January, 2016.

This period proved testing when we went through a roller coaster of emotions. We sold the house, everything had been finalised, removals had been arranged for the beginning of September and we planned to spend some weeks in a holiday house in Worthing before moving up to Scotland. That were our plans, with two days to go before moving, our buyers had to withdraw, because their sale fell through. That to us was catastrophically frustrating but as it turned out it proved a merciful providence. It turned out that we were better able to manage Jean's deteriorating health in our home in Cardiff rather than be isolated in a holiday house in Worthing.

Events in the new year progressed quickly, we sold our house and moved up to Edinburgh in the middle of March, staying with the family until we moved into our apartment in Fairmilehead on May 18th, 2016.

Jean's on-going health issues were monitored by NHS Scotland. She received corrective eye surgery on the 7th November, 2016 and her thyroid was removed on Friday, 27th October 2017.

The past four years have confirmed that our decision to uproot from Cardiff was right. We have settled in well in Edinburgh and found in Charlotte Chapel a spiritual home that has made us welcomed and provided opportunities for us to serve. It is a Christ centred, gospel serving community that is at the very heart of the city. It reaches out to the world, living out the great commission of making disciples of all nations.

This phase of life has been a blessing to us. Yes, inevitably we miss certain things about our life in Wales, but we acknowledge God's gracious and loving providence that has brought us to a good place. There is a delight and a joy to see God at work bringing people into his kingdom from the nations of the world and seeing people mature in Christ.

The kindness and love of our genetic family is also a delight. God has put us in families for a purpose. In the words of the prophetic writings: 'Great is your faithfulness'.

Around the Bay of Mull. Jean Fenney.

Dawn light – Ardnamurchan [West of Scotland] Jean Fenney

18

POSTSCRIPT

As I bring this memoir to a close, I reflect on a varied, interesting and blessed life. I am reminded of a chorus that I was taught in my Sunday School days, "Count your many blessings, name them one by one, and it will surprise you what the Lord has done". How beautifully true that is, innumerable blessings that have cascaded from a gracious, loving Father.

Having a Christian perspective enables one to view life through a powerful, life transforming lens. Without it life would be diminished, even appear to be without purpose, using a quote from one that has aggressively advocated an atheistic world view: *"In a universe of electrons and selfish genes, blind physical forces and genetic replication, some people are going to get hurt, other people are going to get lucky, and you won't find any rhyme or reason in it, nor any justice. The universe that we observe has precisely the properties we should expect if there is, at bottom, no design, no purpose, no evil, no good, nothing but pitiless indifference."*[21]

That is a pretty despairing perspective which ultimately leads to a sense of hopelessness. A Christian world view is radically different, it is emancipating and liberating. It enables one to trace the Lord at work in the ordinary things of life as well as the extraordinary. The Psalmist sees God speaking through creation and then through his revealed word, and finally through personal experience [Psa. 19]. What I have rehearsed in this memoir is God at work in the ordinary things of life and an acknowledgment that I am enabled to trace the wondrous and gracious providences of

God. To look at things retrospectively, gives you an insight that you don't have at a specific point in time. It is only when you look back that you begin to see how the jigsaw fits together, you become aware of doors that are opened, or even for that matter shut, and trace the finger of Divine providence. In the words of William Cowper:

God moves in a mysterious way
His wonders to perform
He plants His footsteps in the sea
And rides upon the storm
Deep in His dark and hidden mines
With never-failing skill
He fashions all His bright designs
And works His sovereign will

O fearful saints new courage take
The clouds that you now dread
Are big with mercy and will break
In blessings on your head
Judge not the Lord by feeble sense
But trust Him for His grace
Behind a frowning providence
He hides a smiling face

I have introduced you to Irelian Jones, in an earlier chapter with his quote, "*It is not glory for me, it is glory to Him*". That is so true, as one weighs and evaluates our lives, one must acknowledge that if there has been anything of immediate or eternal consequence, then it is 'glory to Him'.

I leave you to reflect, on a meditation that I gave to the prayer fellowship at Charlotte Chapel in June, 2020.

"*The lockdown has become a blessing. Spurred on by family, I have started to write my memoir, which I have delayed doing until now. My study desk has spilled over to the guest bedroom and then to the dining room, covering them with papers, articles, photographs, documents and artifacts. It has been all consuming.*

I have tumbled out of bed at 2:00 o'clock in the morning, to capture a memory, before it escapes in the mist of the night. I have reconnected with my roots, "Mynydd Mawr" [Big Mountain], the area I was brought up in, which was known during the time of the Welsh revival of 1904 as 'the mountain of the blessing of God'. I have relived my 'Mount Horeb' experience, when I encountered the living flame of the Divine presence which was life transforming and redirecting. Nothing ever could be the same after that, yes, I have stood on holy ground.

For the original, authentic Horeb experience, we need to think of Moses. He is at the backside of a desert, where he encountered the living God, in a bush that burnt but was not consumed and where he received the revelation of the divine name: 'I AM WHO I AM' [Ex. 3:14], a name that resonates in the 'I AM's' of John's gospel. It was here that he was directed to see a great need by the words of YAHWEH; 'I have indeed seen the misery of my people in Egypt, I have heard them crying out because of their slave drivers, and I am concerned about their suffering. So, I have come down to rescue them from the hand of the Egyptians and to bring them up out of that land into a good and spacious land, a land, flowing with milk and honey.' [Ex. 3:7-8]. Here we have God involved with the pain of his people: "seen their misery, heard them crying, concerned about their suffering, coming down to their rescue, bringing them out".

Moses had marked out this moment in the sand of time, for him it was unforgettable. It is as if at this specific point in history 'God remembered' and so we read: 'God heard their groaning and he remembered his covenant with Abraham, with Isaac and with Jacob.' This was the moment when God looked on the Israelites and was concerned about them' [Ex. 2:24-24]. God remembered, God heard, God looked, God was concerned.

God calls Moses, to have a part in this work of rescue and salvation. He was a reluctant 'Saviour', he had a shaft of reasons why it should not be him, but God promised his presence to be with him. This God is always completely true to his name. He would be to Moses, all that he ever needed – 'THE I AM WHO I AM'.

What God was to Moses, he is that to us. Facing unprecedent times with innumerable uncertainties, 'let us draw near to God with sincere heart and with the full assurance of faith' [Heb. 10:22], knowing that amidst our trials, separation, isolation, doubts, confusion and uncertainty God will be to us all that we will ever need, through Jesus Christ our Lord, the I AM of new testament revelation."

So, fix your eyes on Jesus. Make this your passion.

Be Thou my vision, O Lord of my heart,
naught be all else to me, save that Thou art,
Thou my best thought, by day or by night.
waking or sleeping, Thy presence my light.

Be Thou my wisdom, Thou my true word;
I ever with Thee, Thou with me, Lord;
Thou my great Father, I Thy true son;
Thou in me dwelling and I with Thee one.

High King of Heaven, after victory won,
may I reach heaven's joys, O bright heaven's Sun!
Heart of my own heart, whatever befall,
still be my vision, O ruler of all.

APPENDICES

I

CENTENARY SERVICE
EGLWYS EFENGYLEDD, PENYGROES

ADDRESS GIVEN BY DAVID REES
AT THE CENTENARY SERVICE
OCTOBER 23rd, 2010

It is a real privilege to be with you today and be part of this centenary service and to have this opportunity to reflect on some of the history of 'Eglwys Efengyledd', Penygroes.

Today brings back many wonderful memories. I am thankful to God for the part that the church played in my spiritual development. It was here and, in the home, that I first heard the good news of the gospel of our Lord Jesus Christ.

It was here as a young lad on Sunday evening, November 9th, 1958, that I experienced the irresistible call of God in the gospel, when the Lord saved me. It was weekend meetings with the Open Air Mission. It unquestionably was the most significant moment in my life that determined its future course and direction.

It has very much shaped my priorities and choices in life and those of my family. And so, I look back today to the sheer magnificence of God's grace towards us as a family and it is with deep gratitude that I want to put on public record the part that 'Eglwys Efengyledd, Penygroes' has made to that story.

I must confess the task of putting together a coherent narrative of the history of the fellowship has been challenging. The principle reason is the lack of historical documents to refer to. Hindsight is a wonderful thing. How, I regret that I didn't ask my Father, to document some of the key events of those earlier years.

How did the fellowship come about? That is a good place for us to start. We cannot answer that question without first appreciating the impact of the 1904 revival on Penygroes and its people.

Here I am indebted to my brother in law, Ronnie Perkins, who drew my attention to a book published in Welsh in 1924, entitled: 'Diwrnod yn y Winllan' – a day in the vineyard'[1].

This is a biography of Rev. William Bowen, who had completed 25 years of happy ministry at the Congregational chapel in Penygroes and Milo by February, 1905. The book is written by his son, Rev. D. Edgar Bowen. Ronnie very kindly translated some of the book into English for me. This book for me was indispensable to appreciate the development of the revival in Penygroes.

Here I quote from this book.

Before the revival broke out for years there had been a continual increase in the numbers and the strength of the church in Penygroes. Large numbers gathered on the Sunday, so much so that the building was insufficient for the purpose.

There was a desire for the greater things they had heard of in other parts. Like scores of other churches in Wales, the church at Penygroes went on its knees before God to pray for a greater outpouring of the Holy Spirit in her life and work.

The outcome was that over a period of months, the village was shaken to its foundations by the mighty wind from heaven. The saving power of God's Spirit at work in the souls of men profoundly affected the community.

An eye witness account: *'We have seen in many gatherings men bowed to the ground by the intense atmosphere, their hearts broken and themselves crying out for mercy. Some were praying, others were praising, the tears streaming down their cheeks and their faces shining as the sun.*

We remember seeing drunkards coming in drunk to the services and going out sober – some of whom remain to this day as pillars of God's grace.'

Dr Gwylfa Roberts, Llanelli *– I came to Penygroes, Congregational Chapel, with the intention of preaching in the afternoon and evening. This was an arrangement made long before. However, when I arrived in the afternoon there was no way of entering the chapel because it was so full. I had the greatest difficulty in trying to reach the 'set fawr'.*

The people were sitting in the aisles as much as in the seats. They were shouting and weeping and jumping and praying – all at the same time – and Mr Bowen the minister sitting in the 'set fawr' looking at them with no hope of getting silence.

Here was a living fire giving light, a congregation aflame; men, and even their tears were like clear flames on their cheeks.

As to their prayers, well! That is not what they were if judged by anything I had experienced before. It was lament and laughter, singing and spontaneous praying, and all of this mixed together in one. Some lay on the floor, others spoke loudly interrupting others. Verses were also recited and the service was both a flood and a cleansing place for all.

It was an unearthly commotion! I have never seen anything like it and it was impossible to think of preaching that afternoon. It was a little quieter by the evening; the service had lost the spontaneity of the afternoon and was happy, with people rejoicing. It was a day I will never forget!

Many other testimonies similar in nature could be adduced from the recollections of other ministers who were present at other services in Penygroes. Indeed, the whole area quickly became known as *'the mountain of the blessing of God'.*

A quote from a letter, written by a layman to Rev. Bowen, dated April 1906, a year and a half after the outbreak of the Revival. It gives an important insight into some of the tensions emerging because of the revival.

'You at Penygroes have been blessed with spiritual blessings beyond others. I am glad that you as the shepherd of the church *have allowed the Holy Spirit to work his own way on the people. You have been blessed with wisdom from above and you will be forever thankful that you have not been a supporter of 'the children of Lot' in the battle between light and darkness. I am very glad that you, a minister, have received of the influences of the Revival and that you are gracious to her children'.*

Clearly, from this letter you can see that there were two camps emerging, one that was supportive of the revival and others that were detractors. William Bowen, was very supportive and defended its principles, but sadly suffered as a result of this.

Eventually this led to a parting of the ways, and on Whit Sunday 1913, William Bowen and his followers made Mynudd Seion, a new congregational church, their spiritual home.

If on the one hand there were tensions, on the other hand there was the blessing of the bringing together of God's people, across denominational divides.

This meant that new converts, and established Christians who had been renewed by God's Spirit, met together for prayer and praise at the Congregational schoolroom, under the leadership of William Bowen.

Many of the new and revitalised Christians were increasingly feeling that the historic denominations were resisting the exuberance and joy of the new converts. The establishment, as they were seen, were asserting control of the main services, marginalising the influence of the children of the revival.

Dr Eifion Evans in his book, 'The Welsh Revival of 1904'[2], referring to the factors that led to the secession writes: *'the ecstasy of the new wine was all too soon curbed by the frigidity of the old bottles'.*

In July, 1907, many Christians who had been deeply affected by the revival, from the various chapels in Penygroes and district, attended the 'Keswick in Wales' convention in Llandrindod Wells[3].

In that convention they felt that they had the opportunity to celebrate and express their oneness in the body of Christ, where believers across denominations were able together to worship and joy in God.

This resulted in a number of people resolving that they wanted to express this unity and know this freedom in the context of their regular weekly worship.

This was the germinating seed that brought to birth, 'Eglwys Efengyledd, Penygroes'

A group of believers decided that they wanted the freedom to hear the gospel preached by God's servants, irrespective of their denominational labels.

Some of the names of the people involved were[3]:

Henry Richards (known as Henry Banc) and his wife Susannah.
Ebenezer Griffiths and his wife Elinor [parents of D. T. Griffiths, who was commended to serve God in Poland]
William Roderick
James John
David Daniels and his wife Maryanne
William Rees and his wife Lizzie Ann [Gwenda's grandparents]
David Evans and his wife Ann
David Davies [Pantybas Farm]
Daniel Thomas [Cefnrhiwlas, Penybang, Llandeilo]
Mary Oliver [Ty Canol, Gate Rd]
Catherine Roberts [Ty Uchaf , Gate Rd]
Mrs Hollins [sister of Catherine Roberts] – she lodged with George Muller of Bristol. As an aside I was interested to learn that George Muller, gave a gospel van to evangelise throughout Wales – Willie Evans, from Pontypridd was the full-time worker to man the van.

They initially held cottage meetings during the week, in the evening and on Sunday evening, after the evening service in their own chapels. They met at the home of Henry & Susannah Richards in 4 Dobelle Terrace, Gorslas. Their first meeting was 3rd Sunday in August, 1907[3].

During this period they made the decision to have an independent building and they decided on purchasing a piece of land, which had been part of a quarry and from which Bryncwar road was built. They built the building we are now in, and it became known as 'Mission Gerrig, Penygroes[3].'

Initially, its purpose was as a replacement to using No 4 Dobelle Terrace, Gorslas. I imagine that the reason for this was the numbers attending had outgrown the room available.

They at this stage had still not decided to establish an independent church. However, very shortly afterwards, it was decided to open it as a mission hall, with an independent congregation.

The congregation was quite large, so a vestry, porch and baptistery was added, together with a coal and wood burner located inside the main building. The full plot as we know it today was squared up and purchased. Additionally a plot of land was purchased in Gate Rd to be used as a burial ground and named Machpelah; named after the plot where Abraham buried his wife[3].

A Trust Deed for the Mission hall was drawn up in Welsh and is dated 14th Oct. 1909[4,5]

It makes very interesting reading. I will summarise it under three headings. The mission hall was to be:

A Gospel centred church: *'Inasmuch as this Mission Hall was originally built for a specific purpose namely to preach the Gospel of our Lord and Saviour Jesus Christ and evangelise'*

A Bible based church – its authority scripture: *'There shall be perfect liberty to worship in Spirit and in Truth in accordance with the Written Word of God.'*

Non-sectarian church: *'Regarding the holding of Special Services, there is liberty to call and engage an accredited Servant of God who is a Minister of the New Testament, whether he be a Pastor, a minister of the Church of England, or any lay brother or person provided his life accords with his profession and that he has a vital testimony witnessing to the saving grace of God in salvation'.*

So, the evangelistic hall was established to proclaim Christ and his gospel, to be faithful to scripture in terms of its worship, teaching and service and be catholic in spirit, embracing all people who confess Jesus Christ as Lord.

Invariably, when God is at work the devil is active to hinder and destroy and that is how it turned out to be.

There was an early division. The believers that had come out of the chapels had a range of sympathies. There was a significant Pentecostal group in the Hall which was influenced by Cecil Pollil[6]. After separating from the Hall, they were shaped in part by W. O. Hutchinson of Bournemouth, founder of the Apostolic Faith Church[6].

Division took place in 1913. The trustees locked the gates of the Hall one Sunday in the early part of 1913 and those sympathetic to the Pentecostal position had to hold their meetings elsewhere.

An interesting perspective is given by Rees Evans[6, 9], where he records that *'going to the services on a Sabbath morning, behold there was a locked door with double locks awaiting us. The old Mother earth was dressed in white with snow. Therefore we had to hold our service under the canopy of heaven in the Temple of nature'*[10].

In his book 'On the wings of the Dove', Noel Gibbard gives the view that, *'the local people looked upon the event as a clash between two revival groups – those that advocated free worship and the 'pentecostal dancers'.*[7]

The group that went out initially met in a room in the Council school, and later they acquired a plot of land, directly opposite 'Eglwys Efengylaidd', and built a hall which they called 'Pabell y Cyfarfod' (Tabernacle of the Congregation)[11].

Following the visit of W. O. Hutchinson of Bournemouth, who was described as an Apostle, the new church set apart two brothers in the flesh, D. P. Williams (Pastor Dan) and W. Jones Williams, one to be an Apostle and the other a Prophet. This was done after anointing them with oil, and the laying on of hands, declaring them to be over the little Nation, that is the Welsh nation. [12]

In every respect the group that went out were orthodox, except when it came to the exercise of charismatic gifts and their view on 'the perseverance of the saints'.

Their particular distinctive on the charismatic gifts were the appointment of apostles and prophets, acceptance of the supernatural gifts of the Spirit, including speaking with Tongues and baptism with the Holy Spirit, as a separate experience to conversion.

When you see historically how the work of God has developed since then, you recognise that the devil often overreaches himself in situations like this. The Lord graciously overrules our foolishness and the outcome is the furthering of the work of God in the world.

Let us now look at a few of the human stories.

Here I bring to you a personal and very limited perspective, which in part stems from the fact that I have been away from Penygroes since 1965.

The fire of revival brought into being a number of independent missions that were characterised by an incredible warmth and passion for the Lord and his gospel.

The children of the revival had a deep, genuine devotion to the Lord and were committed to the reading and study of the scriptures and they were bold in their witness for Christ. They took seriously their call to be His witnesses.

I have hardly any memories of the founding members, apart from recognising some of their names. There are however memories of certain long-established members.

Harry Lewis: My memory of Harry was the way he prayed. Often, as he rehearsed the great blessings of the gospel, he used to break out into the 'hwyl'. As a young man growing up in the Hall, I was mesmerised by this. You had this cascade of praise, rushing out like a torrent, modulated by a rhythmic serenade, with a heart that was delighting in God.

Maggie Oliver. Maggie had drunk very deeply from the stream of revival and was captivated by the importance of being on fire for the Lord. She used to wear a hat and carry a handbag with verses of scripture on them.

By the time I was a teenager she had moved to Carmarthen, but whenever I met her she always asked me; 'Dafydd bach a wyt di ar tan dros yr Arglwyth' – David, are you on fire for the Lord. That was quite an intimidating question to a young Christian trying to find his feet!

Arwyn Davies, Lot-Wen. Arwyn and his good friend Meurig Thomas where individuals who loved the Lord and wanted to serve Him. Meurig was a member of the mission hall in Llandysul. They went out together, regularly on a Saturday to preach the gospel in the open air to the villages of Carmarthenshire, and I remember going with them a few times as a young man.

Both suffered from a slight stammer, Meurig's was more pronounced than Arwyn's, but this did not deter them from preaching, such was their love of the Lord and passion for the lost.

Arwyn, married later in life, Meurig's sister, Blodwen. I will never forget the first Sunday morning, after they had returned from their honeymoon, Arwyn shared a meditation from the Song of Solomon.

This book is part of the wisdom literature of Scripture and celebrates the theme of love. It can be understood as a celebration of marital love, or seen as an allegory that describes God's love for his people. He prefaced his remarks with the words: *'that he had only just begun to understand this book!'*

Lewis Rees, my own father had a wonderful conversion story. He would have been quite a young child when the 1904 revival occurred; nevertheless, he imbibed something of the spiritual atmosphere of the period.

It was not until his late twenties, that God broke into his life. He was then a married man, a father of two sons, both of whom died from pneumonia before they were barely into their first year of life.

He decided, and the reason for this decision to me is unclear, to go down to Carmarthen, travelling in a charabanc, with a number of believers from Mission Cerrig, who were going there to hold an open-air witness to proclaim the gospel.

My brother's Peter memory of this was that he had gone down to play rugby and ended up after his conversion by throwing his rugby kit into the river Towy. That is a great story but I am not sure whether it is completely true.

The one fact that is certain is that he did attend the open-air service, which was held in Carmarthen Square, in front of what was then the Council building. It was here that the light of the gospel dawned on him, when he passed from darkness into light, and Lewis was never the same again.

The journey down in the charabanc was eventful in that it went off the road beyond Tumble. Lewis's take on this in later life was that behind that accident there was a sinister hand, the devil himself, who did his utmost to hinder Lewis Rees attend the open-air meeting.

However, God's purpose could not be thwarted; there was no power on earth or in hell that could have changed the appointment that Lewis Rees had with the Lord, at Carmarthen square.

His destiny had already been determined; his name was in the Lamb's book of life, written there by divine decree from eternity past. So what took place at Carmarthen Square, was his meeting with destiny, when God's mercy was poured into his life.

My brother, John, who passed away August this year, recalled occasions when growing up, he would go down with Dad shopping in Carmarthen, and there was not an occasion when Lewis didn't go to Carmarthen Square and bow the knee to thank God for 'seeing the light' [John's words].

The reality of what took place in Carmarthen Square powerfully remained with him, shaped his life and determined his priorities. We as children (Ann, Peter, John and David), thank God for godly parents who taught us the gospel. In one of his books that I recently came across, are written the words: 'Saved by Grace' at Carmarthen Square, 18th February, 1922, Lewis Rees.

There are so many memories. I think of the words in Hebrews 11, when the writer speaks of the great people of faith: 'And what more shall I say? for time would fail me to tell of Jack Thomas,

Will Davies, Cecil Leonard, Tom Davies, Austin Davies and of all the sisters, and so on.

A world-wide vision

As we have already seen two of the original members that met in Penygroes, in 1907 were Eben Griffiths and his wife. Eben was one of the leaders from the beginning and continued to lead the non-Pentecostals that met in the Evangelistic Hall. His son David Thomas Griffiths responded to the call to be an overseas missionary. This he did in a meeting in Llanelli on 15th October 1921[13].

This was at a convention meeting. The preachers were Rees Howells (back from Africa), founder of Swansea Bible College, and William Fetler of Russia. Fetler had travelled via Porth, Rhondda, where he had spoken with R. B. Jones. This was probably his first visit to Wales since the revival period of 1904-05.[14]

After preaching at Llanelli on the Saturday afternoon, William Fetler tested the meeting and nine persons committed themselves to overseas mission. David Thomas Griffiths was one, and another was Sally.

Interestingly, they were R B. Jones's first students at Porth in 1909, where he set up a Bible school. So clearly, they recognised the need for training to be equipped to serve the Lord overseas.

David Griffiths and Sally Evans were soon married and volunteered to work with William Fetler's Russian Missionary Society. In 1921 the Griffiths' left for Baranovitchi, Poland.

In Poland, they eventually worked with S. K. Hine and his wife. He is best known for translating from Russian the hymn, 'How Great thou art'. They bought an empty brewery and turned it into a gospel hall, seating about three hundred, and interestingly, at their opening service, in attendance was a local Roman Catholic priest who gave his blessing to the work.[15]

I heard a Polish church leader speaking a few years ago in Cardiff and he thanked Wales for sending out one of its sons, to bring the gospel to Poland, and of course he was thinking of D. T. Griffiths.

Then we have, Mr and Mrs John Dan Rees, who went out as missionaries to Brazil. He was born in Llanddewi Brefi, Cardigan but eventually made his home in Penygroes in 1905. He was converted in 1923, at the age of 18, under the preaching of Clark and Bell.

In 1928 he felt called to serve God on the missionary field. The circumstances that led to this call are worth recalling. He attended the missionary convention held at Bethany, Ammanford during Whitsun and when the missionary offering was taken, he had intended to give the loose change in his pocket, but instead felt compelled to give every penny and in the end the offering of himself to the Master's service. He went to the Glasgow Bible Training Institute to prepare himself for Christian service.

In 1932 he went out, with his wife Maggie Maud Griffiths to serve God in Brazil, under the auspices of the Inland South American Missionary Union, which is now known as 'New Testament Missionary Union. His first wife died in 1937, and he married again in 1940, an American missionary, Margaret.

He served on the missionary field for 54 years and was called home to be with the Lord, who he had faithfully served in 1985. His wife passed away in 1998.

He worked in the south west state of Mato Grosso do Sul, in a church planting ministry, first among the Indians, then later among other citizens. He served in the church in Rondonopolis, and then travelled to many towns and villages and planted many churches in the State of Mato Grosso.

Mary Helena, John Dan's daughter in an email I had this month wrote: '*Recently I visited a couple of these churches and they are flourishing*'.

The South American continent has seen considerable growth in the Kingdom of Christ over the past 50 years, and this is par-ticularly true of Brazil. I was delighted to learn that one of John Dan's grandsons, Peter Junior is an elder in a thriving congrega-tion in the capital, Campo Grande.

Only in eternity will we be able to see what God has wrought through the service of people like John Dan Rees and D. T.

Griffiths and the contribution that Eglwys Efengyledd, Penygroes has made to the cause of Christ internationally.

In terms of the on-going story of the Gospel ripples that have flown out of Mission Cerrig, I think of some of the grandchildren. I have already mentioned John Dan's grandson. I think of others. Here I am sure my knowledge is probably very incomplete, but I can think of at least four grandchildren who are now engaged in full-time Christian work.

These are people who have a significant Christian ministry, who are Christ centred, gospel people, passionate to make Christ known. One is the grandson of Cecil Leonard, [Mair Davies son, Peter] and then three are the grandsons of Lewis Rees, our sons.

I will just expand briefly on one of these because of the link to the Welsh revival, which brings this overview, a full-circle from where I started.

Paul Lewis Rees, our eldest son is Senior Pastor at Charlotte Chapel Edinburgh and Charlotte Chapel was deeply affected by the Welsh revival. Here is a short quote from a book published by Charlotte Chapel of its history.[16]

Joseph Kemp, the minister of Charlotte chapel, returned from Wales on Saturday 22 January 1905. He brought with him a colleague from Wales, Mr Thomas, to assist him in describing what had been happening there. The regular monthly Saturday conference was already in progress when they walked down the aisle of the Chapel.

The people listened eagerly to what Joseph Kemp had experienced in the Welsh Revival and its effect on his own soul. After telling the story, he tested the meeting, asking if there was anyone who wanted to be saved. About five seats from the front a man rose, saying: 'I want you to pray for me.' He was the first of hundreds to be saved over the next few months, as Revival came to Charlotte Chapel, starting on Saturday 22 January 1905. The conference lasted from 3.30 p.m. until after midnight; the fire of God fell – the prayers of many months were answered.[16]

The chapel today is still numerically a very strong church, championing the cause of the gospel in Edinburgh, Scotland and internationally.

What then about today. Wales of today and Penygroes of today are very different from that at the beginning of the 20th century. There is a great spiritual need, ours is a time of indifference and impoverishment. Men are lovers of pleasure more than lovers of God. The church is weak and is only a shadow of its former glory.

Today is not the occasion to analyse the reasons for this weakness but sufficient to say that for me preparing for today has been both a great blessing and humbling as I have been reminded of the glory of former days.

I think of the American, Jonathan Edwards who was used by God in the great awakening in American early in the 19th century. He was a great preacher with a giant intellect and deep godliness, who recognised that in times of revival there was the authentic and the artificial, the true and the false, side by side. He wrote a book on the 'Religious Affections' to help people to distinguish between the two.

He modelled for us Christian faithfulness in a post-revival period where he emphasised three things. First, the importance of biblical preaching, second, to focus on the basics of building local churches and third he encourages us to know the empowering of the Holy Spirit as we serve God.[17] It is important to be reminded of this as we serve God in our generation.

Wayne Grudem, research professor on Theological and Biblical studies at Phoenix Seminary did a lecture tour of the UK in June of this year, where he spoke on the question: 'Does political involvement distract from the gospel'.

He drew his lecture to a close with some encouraging insights. He made the observation that there has been significant growth in the world of Bible believing Christians, since the 1950's from around 3% to currently around 12%. This growth has mainly come from Africa, Asia and Latin America.

He then posed the question: *'What about Europe and North America? Will God bring revival to all the other countries of the world and pass by this nation, this continent- this nation that has brought so much blessing to the world, from the truths of the reformation to the translation of the Bible into English. I hope not. Revival is yet coming, I think so'*[18].

The lesson from history is that God visits his people in revival when his people humble themselves before him in prayer. Psalm 80 is an appropriate prayer for us to make at this centenary, as I bring this part of the service to a close:

'Give ear, O shepherd of Israel, you who lead Joseph like a flock! You who are enthroned upon the cherubim, shine forth. Stir up your might and come and save us! 'Restore us, O God; let your face shine, that we may be saved! Amen.

David Rees, Cardiff

23rd October, 2010

1. D. Edgar Bowen: 'Diwrnod yn y Winllan' - Cofiant y Parch. W. Bowen, Penygroes a Milo gan ei Fab y Parch. D edgar Bowen; Guilford ac Ebraill, 1924 [Held at University of Aberstwydd Wales National archive.]
2. Eifion Evans: 'The Welsh Revival of 1904' Evangelic Movement of Wales Press, 1969.
3. Eglwys Efengyledd Document: Document held by the Secretary [John Protheroe Thomas] and written by one of the original founding members, not dated but written post 1910.
4. The original Trust document was in Welsh and consisted of the first six paragraphs. The 7th paragraph appears to be a later amendment to the document which is reflected by the date 1958. The one name on the original version was: Arwyddwyd ar rhan yr YMDDIRIEDOLWYR, Rees Evans. Cadeirydd, ac Ysgrifennyd.
5. Brymor Pierce Jones: 'How Lovely Are Thy Dwellings', Wellspring, 1999. This document appears as Appendix A in this book.
6. Pastor Rees Evans: 'Precious Jewels –From the 1904 revival in Wales' Published by J. W. Thomas and Sons, County Press, Llandeilo.1962, p8.
7. Noel Gibbard: 'On the Wings of the Dove – The international effects of the 1904-05 Revival', Bryntirion Press, 2002, p205.

8. Rees Evans, was a trustee of 'Eglwys Efengylaidd' Penygroes, and was one of the original twelve trustees. He was the chairman and secretary of the trustees that set up the original trust.[4] He clearly identified with the Pentecostal group, as he was one of the members that left to set up what eventually became the Apostolic Church. He became one of the first overseers at the Babell. Interestingly and somewhat surprisingly he did not remain with the Apostolic Church, but eventually returned to the original chapel that he was a member of before the mission came into existence. I say surprisingly, because in his booklet 'Precious Jewels', he is extremely critical of those in the leadership of 'Eglwys Efengylaidd' who resisted the new Pentecostal faction and also critical of the leadership of the chapel that resulted in many of the children of the revival leaving the chapel. On returning he eventually became a deacon. He is probably best known in his death, in that his funeral made national headlines with the words: 'The man who spoke from the dead'. He had previously recorded his own funeral address, which was to be played at his funeral. This happened to the great astonishment of the mourners.

9. Pastor Rees Evans: 'Precious Jewels –From the 1904 revival in Wales' Published by J. W. Thomas and Sons, County Press, Llandeilo.1962, p10.

10. *Ibid*, p8

11. *Ibid*, p10.

12. *Ibid*, p11

13. Noel Gibbard: 'On the Wings of the Dove – The international effects of the 1904-05 Revival' Bryntirion Press, 2002, p207.

14. *Ibid*, p207

15. *Ibid*, p208

16. Kemp, *Joseph W. Kemp*, p. 30. Charlotte Chapel Book 2008.

17. Josh Moody: 'The God-centred Life - insights from Jonathan Edwards for today' IVP 2006, p50

18. Wayne Grudem: 'Does 'political' involvement distract from the gospel?' DVD, The Christian Institute, June, 2010

II

EAST CARMARTHENSHIRE'S MISSION HALL SAINTS

RONNIE PERKINS

This article was originally published in the Welsh language under the title 'Saint y Neuaddau' in 'Y Cylchgrawn Efengylaidd', Spring, 1997. The author confesses that he considers this effort as a cumbersome and, at times, clumsy attempt at translation. The context of the original publication was the preparations for the celebration of the jubilee of the Evangelical Movement of Wales.

A number of dangers face Christians of every age who know God's favour and presence in a new, real and fresh way. One of these is the tendency (albeit an unconscious tendency) to devalue and discount the works of the same God in the period before the greater blessing. (This may well be because of our fallen inclinations to go for the sensational and to fail to realise that all God's works are glorious.) We need, at all times, to seek to avoid that pride of heart that insists that it is only OUR input into God's cause in our, or any generation that is of real worth.

We have an example of this in the Great Awakening of the 18th century in Wales. That greatest of Welsh hymn writers, William Williams, Pantycelyn, in his elegy to his fellow reformer Howell Harris speaks of Wales prior to the awakening, as 'lying in a dark and death like sleep with neither a presbyter, vicar or bishop awake! We can gladly excuse the reconstruction of history by this grieving genius as long as we appreciate that he was engaged in poetic licence and hyperbole.

Whatever may have been the truth in relation to the bishops was not Griffith Jones an example of a vicar faithfully serving his Saviour in Llanddowror? And, although the term 'presbyter' would not have been acceptable to them the same was true of those enthusiastic Nonconformists Philip Pugh in Cardiganshire and Edmund Jones at Pontypool.

It will be a valuable and joyous exercise during 1998 to trace the mercies of the Lord towards our nation from the late '40's onwards when the E.M.W. was formed. There are many of us who have much reason to bless God for the rich inheritance that we have now entered by the efforts of those early pioneers.

The special burden of this article, however, is to seek to redress the balance of reformed evangelical thought that tends to maintain that our land was a total spiritual wilderness from the period following the ebb-tide of the blessing in the first decade of this century until the late '40's. The words of Paul at Lystra are apposite at this point: 'Nevertheless He left not Himself without witness'. Acts 14:17

It is true that the names I will refer to will be unfamiliar to the majority of the readers of the 'Cylchgrawn'. Whilst they are common surnames to any Welsh speaker they retain an anonymity and impersonal air to those who never met them: Eber Griffiths; Billy James, Dafydd Daniel; Alcwyn Oliver; Lewis Rees, Will Davies, Idwal Lewis, Glyndwr Lewis, Edward Hughes, Edward Wilkins, John Dan Jones. We could easily imagine these names appearing as characters in any volume by Daniel Owen (an eminent Welsh novelist of the 19th century). These people, however, were not imaginary characters but men raised up by God to be leaders in new born and distinctive churches.

They were planted in the area surrounding 'Y Mynydd Mawr' (broadly speaking the industrial region of South East Carmarthenshire from Crosshands in the west to Brynaman in the east and on to Glamorganshire); the area of the coal pit and stone quarry. They were located historically in the period that spans the revival of '04 and the period following the end of the Second World War.

Amazing as it seems to us who know, love and live in the area today this was church planting on a major scale. There was a church or preaching station in most of the villages of the area outlined above and others such as Pencoed, Bynea and Cynheidre as pelicans in the wilderness outside the specific area but an essential part of the same fellowship of believers.

WHO WERE THEY?

Lest we misunderstand the situation these were not evangelical churches as we know them today. Although the lettering above the hall where these believers met in Penygroes states in the Welsh language EVANGELICAL CHURCH 1910 A.D. I have the distinct feeling that those good, sober, sedate members of contemporary evangelical churches would have the fright of their lives if they could be transported to any of their meetings. According to many eyewitnesses still alive it would be true to say that the vitality of the new life they had received was so real that it 'boiled over' from time to time. And although, to the best of my knowledge, there was never a serious problem among them with regard to speaking in tongues it would be a fair assessment to suggest that they were more like the church at Corinth than Laodicea. (On looking back, it is true to say that there was a problem with women speaking in the church at Corinth also!).

By any standard these were not formal churches or those of the 'middle of the road' variety. On the other hand, they could not be classed with the Pentecostal and Apostolic churches (which were also to be found in the same locality). This much is clear from the fact that many of the founder members of the Apostolic Church in Penygroes had left the 'evangelical church' already referred to.

The lettering above the main doors in Maesybont and Tycroes give us a clearer idea as to where we may locate the testimony of these saints on the spiritual map of Wales. The lettering in both cases is GOSPEL (or EVANGELISTIC) HALL and, in the case of

Maesybont the date 1923 appears whilst in Tycroes it is 1932. The variant 'evangelistic' is given above since the original lettering is in the Welsh language – NEUADD EFENGYLU – and literally means Hall for evangelising!). They were known colloquially as MISSION HALLS although there is a delightful instance in Brynaman of a godly woman known as Mrs Thomas Gospel!

The fact that the words appear in the Welsh language at Tycroes and Maesybont serves to remind us that it was from the ordinary Welsh speaking folk of the area that these causes received their support.

Unfortunately, (and I use this word advisedly and deliberately for it seems to me that along with the Anglicising I refer to below came a diminishing and, eventually, the demise of the warmth and spontaneity of testimony and expression of worship) the Anglicising of these assemblies of God's people was already at work during this period. We see an example of this in the work of a contemporary wag by the name of Eirwyn Pontsian. He relates in his anecdotal autobiography 'Hyfryd Iawn' how he was persuaded when working underground in one of the pits near Cross Hands to go to the 'Gospel Hall' to a prayer meeting. These are his remarks on the event, 'The thing that struck me as strange was this – they thought I was a worthy subject for their prayers. Personally, I felt that they, also, were a matter for prayer and for this reason that, although they were, every one of them Welsh speaking Welshmen they were praying in English! It might be salutary for us to remember the words of the Lord in Luke 16:8 'For the children of this world are in their generation wiser than the children of light'.

ORIGINS

From where did they come? Although the roots of the cause at Ammanford (which, in some ways could be described as 'mother church' of many of the surrounding halls) go back as far as the closing years of the 19th century, it is true to say that generally speaking, the people of the Halls were the offspring of the '04 Revival. They were people who had been plucked as brands from the burning. The words of one eminent leader among them,

Dafydd Daniel of Tycroes would be echoed in the experience of the majority, 'You may say what you wish, I have been saved. I am on the way to heaven. I still feel the power of the resurrection within my soul. I was transported from death into life that very night. (Excerpt from a taped account of the '04 Revival given in 1958 at Maesybont.) And as others were added to their number over the years eg. Lewis Rees, Irelian Jones, Idwal Lewis, Haydon Jones (the list could be easily lengthened) they too would claim that they had been saved in the same way.

Why, then, did they not stay in the chapels or churches in which many of them had been members and some of them officers? The question is pertinent as there are examples of others who knew the same conversion experience who remained within their original denominational allegiance and knew the Lord's favour. Sadly, they and their gospel were no longer welcome in many of those chapels and churches. As many of them were forced to leave for this reason it was most natural for them to seek fellowship with each other. As time progressed and under the authority of God's word and Spirit these fellowships eventually formed the basis for separate churches.

Thankfully, we have a vivid record of the kind of thing that happened following the Revival in the form of a lecture given by Eddie Wilkins of the Gospel Hall, Cross Hands, some years before his death in 1996. Eddie Wilkins was a sterling example of a Christian gentleman in the garb of a common worker with the marks of Divine grace seen clearly in his life. He served his Saviour with a dignity and faithfulness in his native village that few can match. Here is part of his assessment of the situation: 'The Hall is the fruit of the Revival of 1904-05 and was established in the year 1907. The Revival broke out in Wales, and the area of the 'Mynydd Mawr' – Tumble, Cross Hands and Penygroes – experienced the mighty powers of the Holy Spirit of God. Some 400 people and maybe more were converted during that Revival. There were churches (by and large he is referring to the Welsh Nonconformist chapels here) in favour and others which were divided on the subject. It was thus in this area. Those converted in the Revival had to search for a place to worship. There was a farmer by the name of Thomas Jenkins who lived at Glanlasnant in the valley behind Bryn Seion. He was an erstwhile opponent of the Revival but, having come to the experience of faith, he prepared the barn on his farm, and it was there the people came to worship? (My translation)

Mr Wilkins goes on in his lecture to refer to the connection of the fledgling church with the Gospel Hall at Ammanford and of the kindness and service done by William Herbert of that cause towards the saints at Cross Hands.

Another example of how things were at the time comes from Maesybont. There were two brothers, Richard and Dafydd Perkins, who were converted during the Revival. They were members of Cefnberach Calvinistic Methodist Chapel but, because of their testimony to the grace of God in the Gospel, were finally told by the leaders that it was better for them to go to those who 'believed as they did' rather than 'disturb the chapel'. Anecdotal family evidence suggests that they were, indeed, 'disturbers' in Israel. On one occasion as a preacher in the course of his sermon made, in their view, some heretical statements, one of them got up and in a loud voice said, 'The cockerel is crowing!'.

CHARACTERISTICS

What were some of the characteristics of their life and fellowship together?

- LOVE

This was two-fold – a passionate love for God and the Lord Jesus Christ and a warm love for each other. The first could be seen as they kept the Lord's Supper each Lord's Day and the second in the great concern they had for each other. A further example was that the sisters would invariably greet each other with a holy kiss each time they met.

- JOY

We shall see a different side to these gatherings of the Lord's people as we proceed. This much, however, is clear – there was a profound joy underlying such meetings. Their joy was not limited to the public congregation either. Mrs Powell, Garreg-goch Maesybont was well known in the locality for breaking into songs of praise to the Lord as she travelled on the bus to the market.

I can well remember Lewis Rees of Penygroes interjecting 'Bendigedig' into his powerful preaching, thus indicating the sheer joy he felt in his heart.

- WARMTH

It is reported of William Paxton in his remarks to A.A. Hodge on his inauguration at Princeton USA in 1877, that he said, 'Give them theology, give them orthodoxy, give them exposition...give them learning, but GIVE IT TO THEM WARM'.

It was certainly true of these saints that they were 'fervent in the spirit'. The following expression and others could be heard constantly and consistently in the services: 'Amen', 'Praise the Lord', 'Hallelujah'. (As a footnote is it not passing strange with all our vaunted knowledge and understanding and recovery of Biblical truth such expressions as these are missing from our midst?).

- AN UNQUENCHABLE DESIRE TO SEE OTHERS COMING TO KNOW JESUS CHRIST
  - ➢ By personal testimony in word and life.
  - ➢ By public testimony

i. Groups of them would take any and every opportunity to carry Scripture text banners and distribute tracts in public places. Favourite venues were the seasonal fairs at Llanddarog, Llandeilo and Carmarthen, although more unusual occasions and opportunities would be seized on. There is a note , for example, in Richard Perkins' diaries of such a witness at the opening of a new bridge across the river Towy at Dryslwyn, Carmarthenshire.

ii. Open-air services. When groups of these saints would come together for whatever reason, be it a trip to the seaside or special services they would grasp the opportunity to preach to the people. (Again, a personal recollection may illustrate the reality of their concern for the lost. It was early 1960's and we, as a family, had gone down to the sea at Llansteffan. We had hardly got our first whiff of the sea air when we were greeted by the unique Irelian Jones who was there for the same purpose. On seeing the large number of people, however, Irelian's first remark to my father was, 'we must have an open-air meeting').

The company of other saints was not essential. Eddie Wilkins, Cross Hands, refers to his father, Edward Wilkins, on one occasion preaching on his own at the cross roads at Pontyberem; another time by the row of houses alongside the Stag and Pheasant and many, many times on Cross Hands Square.

Others of similar spiritual calibre were Irelian Jones (already mentioned); Richard Perkins (It was his custom after selling his market garden produce at Llandeilo to preach to the people. His diary entries for the 1920's and 30's reveal that, despite the occasional brush with the police, this was almost a routine occurrence in his weekly life).

iii. Preaching in different homesteads and farms. These were regular Saturday night meetings e.g. in the farms and houses of Maesybont and Llanarthne led by the brethren of Hebron Gospel Hall.

iv. Preaching in the Halls. This was an era in Wales when it was the custom for people to come to such places to listen to the Word (Halcyon days!). There were many in the area who had reason to bless the Lord for the mission of 'Clark and Bell' in Ammanford and Penygroes districts in 1923.

Given such an historical context it is not surprising that the verse that faced the preacher on the back wall opposite the pulpit in so many of the Halls in the area was Paul's charge to Timothy 'Preach the Word'. And it is so coincidence either that the verse facing the congregation was 'Repent and believe the Gospel!'

v.   Preaching in marquees during the summer months. These were erected in villages where there was no testimony (or at best only a muted testimony) to the Gospel. The list of villages visited by John Dan Jones and R S (Dickie) Jones (to name only two) during this period is a long and varied one. It has always thrilled me to think that my home village of Llanarthne was one of the venues for the ministry of John Dan Jones and there were evidences that it was a fruitful ministry.

vi. A WORLD-WIDE VISION. The number of missionaries who left for other countries, from this, comparatively small area, is in many respects quite breathtaking. The following incomplete list gives a taste:

Mr & Mrs D. T. Griffiths, Penygroes to Poland
Mr Edward Wilkins, Cross Hands to South Africa for a period from 1908.
Mr & Mrs Watkin Edwards to South Africa
Mr & Mrs John Dan Rees, Penygroes to Brazil
Mr & Mrs D T Morris to Patagonia
Mr & Mrs J. M. Davies, Ammanford to India
Mr & Mr Henry Rees, Llanelli to India

•   THE CONSCIOUSNESS of the Divine requirement for holiness in the lives of His people.
    Their favoured term to describe each other was, significantly, 'saints'.

•   THE JOYFUL ANTICIPATION OF HEAVEN and longing for the Lord's coming.
    Although their eschatological framework was decidedly premillennial this was no academic curiosity for them but a blessed hope and life changing truth.

THEIR HERITAGE

Hard headed realism tells us there is very little left in the area today of their once vibrant testimony. The building they graced with their presence remain and the flame is still alive in the hearts of the godly remnant but an objective analysis would show that flame to be all but extinguished.

- Unlike the major movements of God's Spirit throughout the centuries following the Reformation these people did not leave a body of literature for us to study.

It is possible that notes of their preaching are still extant in some family archives but these, even if they could be collected, would give only a limited idea of their theology and doctrine.

There are some three (or more?) cassettes transposed, in at least two cases from the original reel tapes of the 50's/ early 60's. These are of value in the absence of written records.

A remarkable complete set of diaries by Richard Perkins is also a worthwhile source.

There is one volume, however, bequeathed in the form of a bilingual hymn book 'Hymnau o Fawl' (Hymns of Praise), published (in 1911 in a second edition) by a committee of the Gospel Hall in Ammanford. This contains some of the work of the hymnwriters among them, Olwyn Jones, Ammanford; Edward Hughes, Cross Hands; David Rees Roberts, Llanelli. (The main body of the hymnal is an interesting mix of the great Welsh doctrinal and experimental hymns of the past and the more evangelistic thrust of hymns from the Moody/Sankey era.). As a footnote, it is worthy of note that the original, pre 1911 edition was a slimmer volume containing only hymns relating to the Lord's sufferings, death, resurrection and coming in glory. This was, presumably, published for use at the gatherings to remember the Lord.

The hymn-book is also important because of some of the hymn tunes composed by some of the local brethren with a gift in the field of music.

- They also left their weaknesses and shortcomings as a legacy for us. What movement, linked with sinful men and women, this side of glory has no errors in some particular area? It is not the purpose of this article to expand on these but they have been left for us to identify and avoid if we possibly can.

GODLY FAMILIES. Two families from the fellowship of believers at Maesybont come to mind immediately, viz. the families who lived at Cwm-Hywel and Garreg-Goch farm respectively. The contributions of the two mothers as true 'mothers in Israel' are worthy of particular mention. These two families are only representative of many others both in Maesybont and the surrounding villages.

- A whole area under blessing. Those blessed served the Lord in a specific generation and time period. Who can measure the preservation from evil and Divine judgement that was the portion of that generation because they lived among saints who acted as 'salt and light' in the community?

- LONGING. The greatest legacy they have left to those who had the privilege of knowing them can be expressed in the Welsh word 'hiraeth', or (less successfully) in the English word 'longing'.
  ➤ For the saints as saints. It is not in vain that Hebrews 13:7 reminds us 'Remember them which have the rule over you, who have spoken unto you the Word of God: whose faith follow, considering the end of their conversation'.
  ➤ For the rich blessing proved by them. We do not see areas under blessing today; instead there are whole communities dare we say under Divine Judgement. 'How long, O Lord?'

Let it come, O Lord, we pray Thee
Let the showers of blessing fall.

> For the spiritual atmosphere of the gatherings. How does one explain the concept of something happening? This was, surely, part of the secret of the power of those days.

There was something 'happening' in the services. There can be no doubting the fact that the Holy Spirit's presence was there among God's people. This was evident in the sheer thrill of anticipation when going to a service. 'I was glad when they said unto me, let us go to the house of the Lord'.

On the other hand, there was holy fear present in the anticipation. Joy and fear – these were the two elements that were still present even in the years of the afterglow (i.e. late 1950's, early 1960's).

Once they found themselves in the services, in the epicentre of the spiritual warmth with the Word of God being preached (the operative word is preached, for men such as Irelian Jones, Lewis Rees, Idwal Lewis and his brother Glyndwr were no anaemic 'speakers' but first and foremost preachers of the Word). There was always the expectation of and waiting for something GREATER to happen i.e. the powerful influence of the Holy Spirit convicting and convincing the hearers of the truth.

This, then, is part of their legacy and this is the 'hiraeth' that remains in the heart of all those who cannot forget the echoes of those stirring years.

CONCLUSION

The one great thing about them and their testimony was that they were people of the living God – the God who cannot be trifled with, the God for whom superficiality and coldness in His worship and service are not options, the God who saves from sin and its consequences in hell.

I would contend that the Halls, at least in this area, were a link between the glory of the earlier period of unparalleled blessing during the 18th and 19th centuries and the happier period of recovery of truth that came to Wales with the birth of the Evangelical Movement of Wales and related work in the Colleges and Universities. It is also a fact that many well-known names of leaders in the Welsh speaking constituency today recognise a debt in one way or another to the untarnished testimony of the 'Mission Hall' saints.

The people mentioned at the beginning would be totally unconcerned if you had never heard of them. They would, however, be very much concerned that we all know, love and serve their Saviour and Lord. Indeed, their prayer would be the words of the following hymn which they often sang together,

'All hail the power of Jesus' name,
Let angels prostrate fall,
Bring forth the royal diadem
And crown Him Lord of all.'

III

FAMILY TREES

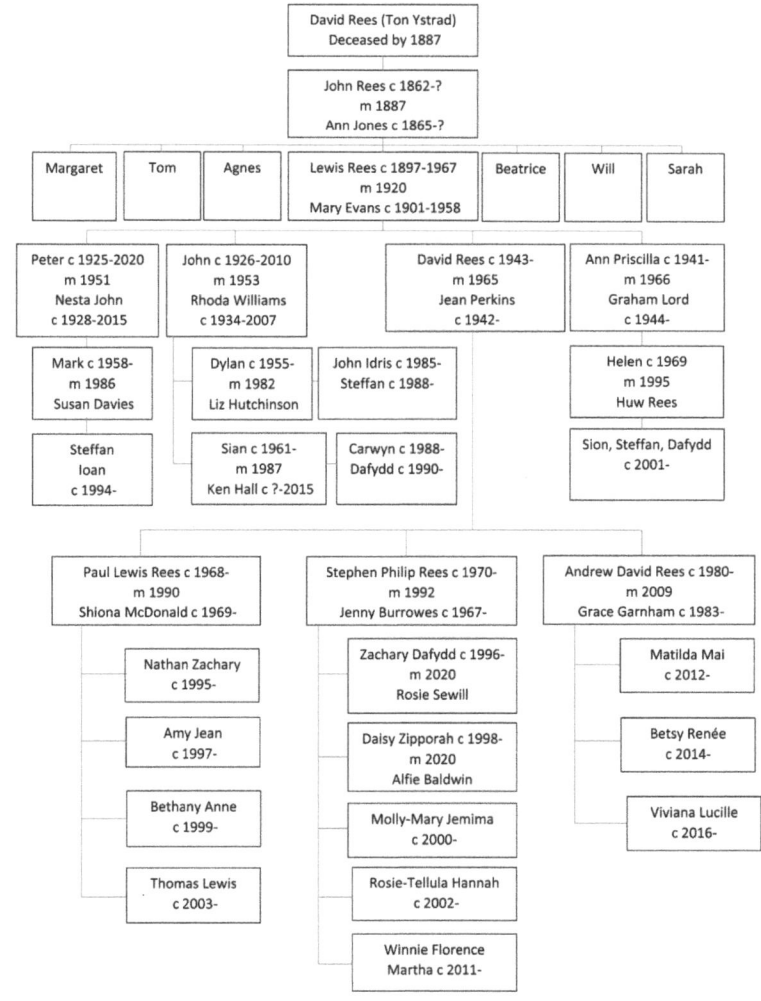

Family Tree of Lewis Rees

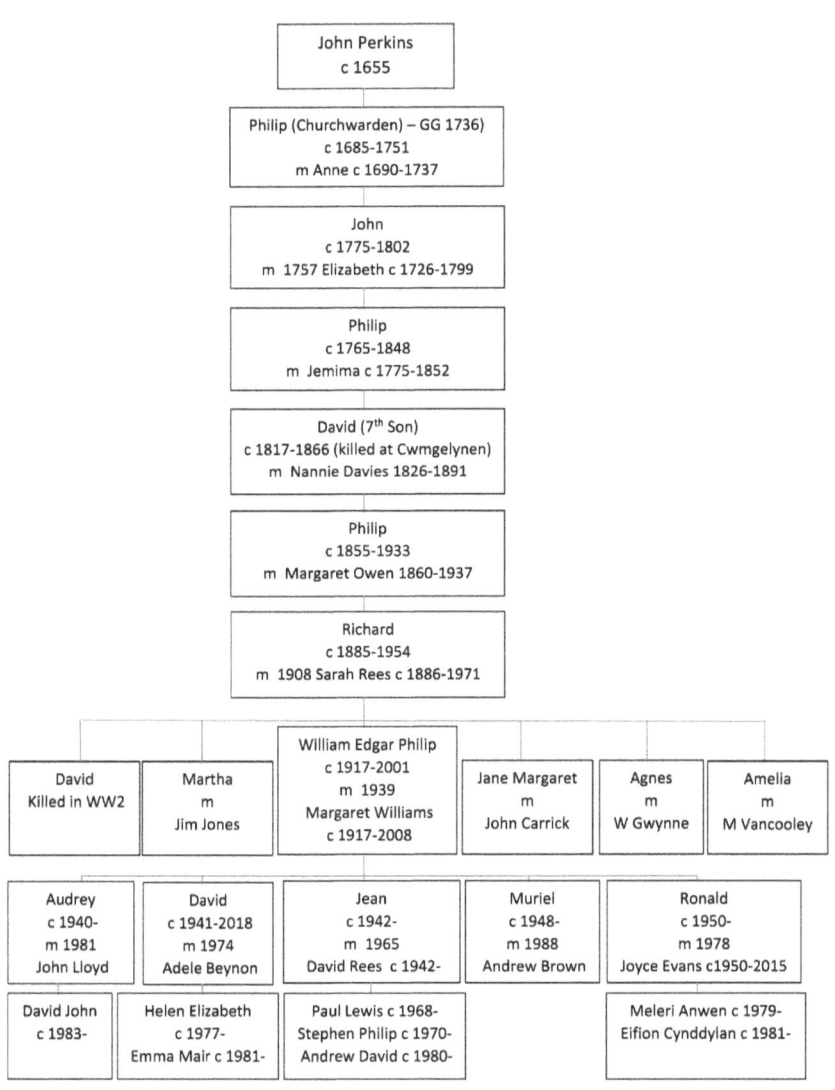

Family Tree of William Edgar Philip Perkins

Based on a version produced by Sidney D Perkins

IV

PUBLICATIONS

Invited Book Chapters

1. Kulikov Gennady G., Haydn A. Thompson (Eds.) Dynamic modelling of gas turbines: identification, simulation, condition monitoring and optimal control – *Springer-Verlag, Advances in Industrial Control Series,* Chapter 5 Linear System Identification, **David Rees** and Neophytos Chiras, April. 2004. ISBN 1852337842.

2. Kulikov Gennady G., Haydn A. Thompson (Eds.) Dynamic modelling of gas turbines: identification, simulation, condition monitoring and optimal control – *Springer-Verlag, Advances in Industrial Control Series,* Chapter 6 Linear Gas Turbine Modelling, David **Rees** and Neophytos Chiras, April. 2004. ISBN 1852337842.

3. Kulikov Gennady G., Haydn A. Thompson (Eds.) Dynamic modelling of gas turbines: identification, simulation, condition monitoring and optimal control – *Springer-Verlag, Advances in Industrial Control Series,* Chapter 8 Nonlinear Gas Turbine Modelling, **David Rees** and Neophytos Chiras, April. 2004. ISBN 1852337842.

4. Gertler Janos J., (Editor) IFAC Annual reviews in control, *Pergamon,* System identification strategies applied to aircraft gas turbine engines, V. Arkov, D. C. Evans, P. J. Fleming, D.

C. Hill, J. P. Norton, I. Pratt, **D. Rees**, and K. Rodriguez-Vazquez, Volume 24, 2000, 67-81.

5. Godfrey Keith (Editor) Perturbation signals for system identification, *Prentice Hall,* Chapter 12 –Design and Application of Non-binary Low-peak-factor Signals for System-dynamic measurement, **David Rees** and David L. Jones, April 1993, ISBN 0-13-656414-3.

6. Barker H. A. (Editor) IFAC Symposia Series, Computer aided design in control systems, *Pergamon*, A digital model for a three-phase induction motor drive using a personal computer software package, C. K. P. Luk, M. G. Jayne, **D. Rees**, D. W. Schaper, 1992, Number 1, 411-416.

7. Jones N. B. and J. D. McK. Watson (editors) Digital signal processing: principles, devices and applications, *Peter Peregrinus*, Chapter 27 – Implementation and performance of digital controllers, **D. Rees**, 1990, ISBN 0 86341 210 6.

8. Warwick K. and **D. Rees** (Editors) Industrial digital control systems (Comprehensively Revised Edition), Chapter 4 – Design of digital controllers, **D. Rees**, *Peter Peregrinus,* 1988, ISBN 0 86341 139 8, 77-114.

9. Warwick K. and **D. Rees** (Editors) Industrial digital control systems (Comprehensively Revised Edition), Chapter 17 A comparison of DDC algorithms – Case study II, **D. Rees**, *Peter Peregrinus, 1988, ISBN 0 86341 139 8, 406-421.*

10. Warwick K. and **D. Rees** (Editors) Industrial digital control systems (Comprehensively Revised Edition), Chapter 18 – Controller implementations using novel processors – Case Study III, **D. Rees** and P. A. Witting, *Peter Peregrinus, 1988, ISBN 0 86341 139 8, 423-449.*

11. Warwick K. and **D. Rees** (Editors) Industrial digital control systems, Chapter 4 – Design of digital controllers, **D. Rees,** *Peter Peregrinus, 1986, ISBN 0 86341 081 2, 71-95.*

12. Warwick K. and **D. Rees** (Editors) Industrial digital control systems, Chapter 17 – A comparison of DDC algorithms

– Case Study II, **D. Rees**, *Peter Peregrinus, 1986, ISBN 0 86341 081 2, 349-365.*

13. Warwick K. and **D. Rees** (Editors) Industrial digital control systems, Chapter 17 – Controller implementations using novel processors – Case Study III, **D. Rees** and P. A. Witting, *Peter Peregrinus, 1986, ISBN 0 86341 081 2, 366-391.*

Edited Books

14. Warwick K. and **D. Rees** (Editors) Industrial digital control systems (Comprehensively Revised Edition), *Peter Peregrinus, 1988, ISBN 0 86341 139 8.*

15. Warwick K. and **D. Rees** (Editors) Industrial digital control systems, *Peter Peregrinus, 1986, ISBN 0 86341 081 2.*

Thesis

16. **Rees D.**, Digital processing of system responses, Ph.D. dissertation, *The Polytechnic of Wales, Faculty of Engineering, Department of Electronics, 1976.*

Journals

1. Sun, J., G.P. Liu, J. Chen and **D. Rees**, Improved delay-range-dependent stability criteria for linear systems with time-varying delays, *Automatica, 2009.*

2. Zhao, Y.B., G.P. Liu and **D. Rees**, Packet-Based Deadband Control for Internet-Based Networked Control Systems, *IEEE Transactions on Control Systems Technology, 2009.*

3. Sun, X.M., G.P. Liu, **D. Rees** and W. Wang, L_2-gain of controller failure for systems with input delay: zero-order hold model, *IEEE Transactions on Control Systems Technology, 2009.*

4. Wang, R., G.P. Liu, W. Wang, **D. Rees** and Y. Zhao, Guaranteed Cost Control for Networked Control Systems

Based on an Improved Predictive Control Method, *IEEE Transactions on Control Systems Technology*, 2009 .

5. Zhao, Y.B., G.P. Liu and **D. Rees**, Modelling and Stabilization of Continuous-Time Packet-Based Networked Control Systems, *IEEE Transactions on Systems, Man and Cybernetics – Part B*, Volume 39, Issue 6, 2009.

6. Zhao, Y.B., G.P. Liu, **D. Rees**, Design of a packet-based control framework for networked control systems, *IEEE Transactions on Control Systems Technology*, vol. 17, no.4, pp. 859-865, 2009.

7. He, Y., G.P. Liu, **D. Rees**, M. Wu. Improved H_infinty filtering for systems with time-varying delay, *Circuits, Systems, and Signal Processing*, 2009.

8. Thanapalan, K.K.T., G.P. Liu, J.G. Williams and **D. Rees**, Robust Fuzzy Controller Development for A PEM Fuel Cell System, *International Journal of Advanced Mechatronic Systems,* 2009.

9. Xia, Y., J. Chen, G.P. Liu, P. Shi and **D. Rees**, Output feedback control of discrete systems with time-varying delay, Dynamics of Continuous, *Dynamics of Continuous, Discrete & Impulsive Systems, Series B: Applications & Algorithms*, 2009.

10. Sun, J., G.P. Liu, J. Chen and **D. Rees**, On improved stability criteria for linear systems with time-varying delay, *IET Control Theory & Applications, 2009.*

11. Sun, J., J. Chen, G.P. Liu and **D. Rees**, Delay-dependent robust h-infinity filter design for uncertain linear systems with time-varying delay, *Circuits, Systems and Signal Processing*, vol.28, no.5, pp. 763-779, 2009.

12. Sun, X.M., G.P. Liu, **D. Rees** and W Wang, Stability analysis for networked control systems based on average dwell time method, *International Journal of Robust and Nonlinear Control*, 2009.

13. Sun, X.M., G.P. Liu, **D. Rees** and W. Wang, Stability analysis for networked control systems based on event-time-driven mode, *International Journal of Control*, Volume 82, Issue 12, pp 2260-2266, Dec. 2009.

14. Xia, Y., J. Chen, G.P. Liu, L. Wang and **D. Rees**, Robust adaptive sliding mode control for uncertain time-delay systems, *International Journal of Adaptive Control and Signal Processing*, vol.23, no.9, pp. 863-881, 2009.

15. Xia, Y., G.P. Liu, M. Fu, and **D. Rees**, Predictive control of networked systems with random delay and data dropout, *IET Control Theory & Applications, 2009.*

16. Chai, S.C., G.P. Liu and **D. Rees**, Design of networked control systems over GPRS wireless networks using the networked predictive control method, *Dynamics of Continuous, Discrete & Impulsive Systems*, 2009 .

17. Ouyang, H., G.P. Liu and **D. Rees**, Robust control of networked predictive control system with perturbation in the nonlinear process, *Dynamics of Continuous, Discrete & Impulsive Systems*, 2009.

18. Wang, R., G.P. Liu, B. Wang, W. Wang, and **D. Rees**, L2-gain analysis for networked predictive control systems based on switching method, *International Journal of Control*, vol. 82, no.6, pp.1148-1156, 2009.

19. He, Y., G.P. Liu, **D. Rees** and M. Wu, H-inf filtering for discrete-time systems with time-varying delay, *Signal Processing*, vol.89, no.3, pp. 275-282, 2009.

20. Sun, J., G.P. Liu, J. Chen and **D. Rees**, Improved stability criteria for neural networks with time-varying delay, *Physics Letter A*, vol. 373, no. 3, pp. 342-348, 2009.

21. Thanapalan, K.K.T., G.P. Liu, J.G. Williams, B. Wang and **D. Rees**, Review and analysis of fuel cell system modelling and control , *International Journal of Computer Aided Engineering and Technology*, vol. 1, no. 2, pp. 145-157, 2009.

22. Xia, Y., J. Chen, G.P. Liu, Peng Shi, Jie Chen and **David Rees**, Robust delay-dependent sliding mode control for uncertain time-delay systems, *International Journal of Robust and Nonlinear Control*, 2007.

23. He Y., G. P. Liu, **D. Rees**, and M. Wu, Improved Delay-dependent Stability Criteria for systems with nonlinear perturbations, *European Journal of Control*, Vol. 13 No. 4, 2007, 356-365.

24. Solomou Michael and **David Rees**, System Modelling and Controller Design in the Presence of Nonlinear Distortions *IEEE Transactions on Instrumentation and Measurement*, VOL 56, No. 3, June 2007.

25. Hu, W. S., G. P. Liu and **D. Rees**, Event –Driven Networked Predictive Control, *IEEE Transactions on Industrial Electronics*, VOL. 54, No. 3, June 2007, 1603-1603.

26. Liu, G.P., Y. Xia, **D. Rees** and W.S. Hu, Design and stability criteria of networked predictive control systems with random network delay in the feedback channel, *IEEE Transactions on Systems, Man and Cybernetics* – Part C: Applications and reviews, VOL. 37, No. 2, March 2007, 173-183.

27. Liu, G.P., Y. Xia, J. Chen, **D. Rees** and W.S. Hu, Networked predictive control of systems with random network delays in both forward and feedback channels, IEEE *Transactions on Industrial Electronics*, Vol. 54, No. 3, June 2007.

28. He, Y., Liu, G.P. and **D. Rees**, New delay-dependent stability criteria for neural networks with time-varying delay, *IEEE Transactions on Neural Networks*, Vol. 18, NO. 1, January 2007, 310-314.

29. He, Y., Liu, G.P. and **D. Rees**, Augmented Lyapunov functional for the calculation of stability interval for time-varying delay, *IET Control Theory Applications*, Vol., 1, No. 1, January 2007, 381-386.

30. Xia, Y., G.P. Liu, P. Shi, **D. Rees** and E.J.C. Thomas, New stability and stabilisation conditions for systems with time-delay, *International Journal of Systems Science*, Vol. 38, No. 1, January 2007, 17-24.

31. Xia, Y., P. Shi, G.P. Liu, **D. Rees**, J. Han, Active disturbance rejection control for uncertain multivariable systems with time-delay, *IET Control Theory Applications*, No. 1, January 2007, 75-81.

32. Ouyang, H., G. P. Liu, **D. Rees** and W.S. Hu, Predictive control of networked non-linear control systems, *Proceedings of IMechE Part I: J. Systems and Control Engineering*, Vol. 221, 2007, 1-11.

33. Xia, Y., P. Shi, **G.P. Liu, D. Rees**, J. Han, Active disturbance rejection control for uncertain multivariable systems with time-delay, IEE Proceedings, Part D -Control Theory and Application, 2006.

34. Xia, Y., **G.P. Liu**, P. Shi and **D. Rees**, Robust delay-dependent sliding mode control for uncertain time-delay systems, *International Journal of Robust and Nonlinear Control*, 2006.

35. Malhotra K., S. Gardner, **D. Rees**, Evaluation of GPRS enabled secure remote patient monitoring system, Arab Health World, June 2006, Vol. XX Issue 3, 23-25.

36. Wang B., **D Rees** and Q-C. Zhong, Control of integral processes with dead time Part IV: various issues about PI controllers, *IEE Proc.-Control Theory Appl.*, Vol. 153, No 3, May 2006.

37. Liu G. P., J. X. Mu, **D. Rees** and S. C. Chai, Design and stability analysis of networked control systems with random communication time delay using the modified MPC, *International Journal of Control*, Vol. 79, No. 4, April 2006, 288-297.

38. Shi Peng, Yuanqing Xia, G. P. Liu, **and D. Rees**, On designing of sliding-mode control for stochastic jump systems, *IEEE*

Transactions on Automatic Control, Vol. 51, No1, January 2006.

39. Liu G. P., **D. Rees**, S. C. Chai and X. Y. Nie, Design, simulation and implementation of networked predictive control systems, *Measurements + Control*, Vol. 38/1 February 2005, 17-21

40. Solomou Michael and **David Rees**, Frequency domain analysis of nonlinear distortions on linear frequency response function measurements, *IEEE Transactions on Instrumentation and Measurement*, Vol. 54, No. 3, June 2005, 1313 – 1320.

41. Mu Junxia, **David Rees** and G P Liu, Advanced controller design for aircraft gas turbine engines, *Control Engineering Practice*, Vol. 13, 2005, 1001-1015.

42. Xia Yuanqing, Guoping Liu, Peng Shi, **David Rees**, Robust mixed H2/H∞ state-feedback control for continuous-time descriptor systems with parameter uncertainties, *Circuits Systems Signal Processing*, Vol. 24, No. 4, 2005, 431-443.

43. Zhong Qing-Chang, **David Rees**, Control of uncertain LTI systems based on an uncertainty and disturbance estimator, *Journal of Dynamic Systems, Measurement, and Control*, Vol. 126, Dec 2004, 905-910.

44. Solomou Michael, **David Rees** and Neophytos Chiras, Frequency domain analysis of nonlinear systems driven by multiharmonic signals, *IEEE Transactions on Instrumentation and Measurement*, Vol. 53, No 2, April 2004, 243-250.

45. Solomou Michael and **David Rees**, Measuring the best linear approximation of systems suffering nonlinear distortions: An alternative method, *IEEE Transactions on Instrumentation and Measurement*, Vol. 52, No. 4 – August 2003, 1114-1119.

46. Chiras N., Evans C., and **Rees D.**, Global nonlinear modeling of gas turbine dynamics using NARMAX structures,

ASME Journal of Engineering for Gas Turbines and Power, Oct 2002, Vol. 124, 817-826.

47. Solomou Michael, Ceri Evans and **David Rees**, Crest factor minization in the frequency domain, *IEEE Transactions on Instrument and Measurement*, Vol. 51, No. 4, August 2002, 859-865.

48. Chiras Neophytos, Ceri Evans, and **David Rees**, Nonlinear gas turbine modelling using NARMAX structures, *IEEE Transactions on Instrumentation and Measurement*, Vol. 50, No. 4, August 2001, 893-898.

49. Evans C., P. J. Fleming, D. C. Hill, J. P. Norton, I. Pratt, **D. Rees**, K. Rodriguez-Vazquez, Application of system identification techniques to aircraft gas turbine engines, *Control Engineering Practice,* Vol. 9, No. 2 Feb. 2001, 135-148.

50. Evans Ceri, and **David Rees**, Nonlinear distortions and multisine signals-Part I: Measuring the best linear approximation, *IEEE Transactions on Instrumentation and Measurement*, Vol. 49, No. 3, June 2000, 602-609.

51. Evans Ceri, and **David Rees**, Nonlinear distortions and multisine signals-Part II: Minimising the distortion, *IEEE Transactions on Instrumentation and Measurement*, Vol. 49, No. 3, June 2000, 610-616.

52. Evans C., **D. Rees**, A. Borrel, Identification of aircraft gas turbine dynamics using frequency-domain techniques, *Control Engineering Practice* Vol. 8, No. 4, April 2000, 457-467.

53. Evans C., A. Borrell and **D. Rees**, Testing and modelling gas turbines using multisine signals and frequency-domain techniques, *ASME Journal of Engineering for Gas Turbines and Power,* July 1999, Vol. 121, 451-457.

54. Evans C., **D. Rees**, and Dave Hill, Frequency domain identification of gas turbine dynamics, *IEEE Transactions on Control Systems Technology*, September 1998, Vol. 6, Number 5, 651-662

55. Weiss Michael, Ceri Evans, and **D Rees**, Identification of nonlinear cascade systems using paired multisine signals, *IEEE Transactions on Instrumentation and Measurement*, Vol. 47, No. 1, February 1998, 332-336.

56. Evans C., **David Rees**, Lee Jones, and Michael Weiss, Periodic signals for measuring nonlinear Volterra kernels, *IEEE Transactions on Instrumentation and Measurement*, Vol. 45, No. 2, April 1996, 362-371.

57. Evans D. C., **D. Rees**, and D. L. Jones, Identifying linear models of systems suffering nonlinear distortions, with a gas turbine application, *IEE Proceedings on Control Theory and Applications*, Vol. 142, Number 3, May 1995, 229-240. *(Publication was awarded the IEE F C Williams Premium for the session 1994/95)*

58. Evans C., **D. Rees**, and L Jones, Nonlinear disturbance errors in system identification using multisine test signals, *IEEE Transactions on Instrumentation and Measurement*, Vol. 43, No. 2, April 1994, 238-244.

59. Evans D. Ceri, **David Rees** and D. Lee Jones, Design of test signals for identification of linear systems with non linear distortions, *IEEE Transactions on Instrumentation and Measurement*, Vol. 41, No. 6, December 1992, 768-774.

60. Morland Gavin, Graham White **and D. Rees**, Rheological data of fibre optic cable filling compounds, *Wire Industry*, April 1992, 343-347

61. **Rees D.**, J. L. L. Roberts, H. Jones, Optical fibre cable design, *Wire Industry*, December 1991, ISSN 0043-6011, 286-290.

62. Sutton P. A., J. L. L. Roberts, A. T. Summers, A. Phoenix and **D. Rees**, Fibre microbend loss mechanism test, *Wire Industry*, March 1990, ISSN 0043-6011, 286-290.

63. **Rees. D.**, Controller Implementation using a monolithic signal processor, International *Journal of Microcomputer Applications*, Vol. 4, No. 3. 1985.

64. Golten J. W., and **D. Rees**, The use of hybrid computing in the analysis of steel rolling, *IEEE Transactions on Electronic Computers*, Vol. EC-16, Number 6, December 1967

Conferences

1. Zhao, Y.B., G.P. Liu and **D. Rees**, Using Deadband in packet-based networked control systems, *Proceedings of the 2009 IEEE International Conference on Systems, Man, and Cybernetics*, San Antonio, pp.2897-2902, 2009.

2. Wang, B., G.P. Liu and **D. Rees**, Networked predictive control of magnetic levitation system, *Proceedings of the 2009 IEEE International Conference on Systems, Man, and Cybernetics*, San Antonio, pp.4200-4205, 2009.

3. Liu, X.P., G.P. Liu, Y.Q. Xia and **D. Rees**, Stability criteria for a class of MIMO networked control systems with network constraints, *Proceedings of the 2009 IEEE International Conference on Systems, Man, and Cybernetics*, San Antonio, pp.4853-4857, 2009.

4. Sun, J., J. Chen, G.P. Liu and **D. Rees**, Stability and stabilization for discrete systems with time-varying delays based on the average dwell-time method, *Proceedings of the 2009 IEEE International Conference on Systems, Man, and Cybernetics*, San Antonio, pp.4931-4935, 2009.

5. Zhao, Y.B., G.P. Liu and **D. Rees**, Stochastic stability analysis of packet-based networked control systems, *Proceedings of the 48th IEEE Conference on Decision and Control*, Shanghai, 2009.

6. Sun, J., J. Chen, G.P. Liu and **D. Rees**, Delay-range-dependent and rate-range-dependent stability criteria for linear systems with time-varying delays, *Proceedings of the 48th IEEE Conference on Decision and Control*, Shanghai, 2009.

7. Sun, J., G.P. Liu, J. Chen and **D. Rees**, Networked predictive control for Hammerstein-Wiener systems via output

feedback, *Proceedings of European Control Conference '09,* Budapest, pp.395-399, 2009.

8. Sun, J., J. Chen, G.P. Liu and **D. Rees,** On robust stability of uncertain neutral systems with discrete and distributed delays, *Proceedings of American Control Conference,* St. Louis, pp.5469-5473, 2009.

9. Li, Peng, G.P. Liu, J. Chen and **D. Rees,** Modelling of fuel cells with voltage degradation, *Proceedings of the 15th International Conference on Automation and Computing,* Luton, pp.131-136, 2009.

10. Yong He, G. P. Liu and **D. Rees,** Improved delay-dependent Stability Criteria for Systems with Nonlinear Perturbations, *Proceedings of the European Control conference 2007,* Kos, Greece, July 2-5, 3311-3317.

11. Hu Wenshan, G. P. Liu and **David Rees,** Network Predictive Control System with Data Compression, *Proceedings of the 2007 IEEE International Conference on Networking, Sensing and Control,* London, UK, 15-17 April 2007, 52-57.

12. Zhao Y. B., G. P. Liu and **D. Rees,** Time Delay Compensation and Stability Analysis of Networked Predictive Control Systems based on Hammerstein Model, *Proceedings of the 2007 IEEE International Conference on Networking, Sensing and Control,* London, UK, 15-17 April 2007, 808-811.

13. Xia Yuanqing, J. Chen, G. P. Liu and **D. Rees,** Stability Analysis of Networked Predictive Control Systems with Random Network Delay, *Proceedings of the 2007 IEEE International Conference on Networking, Sensing and Control,* London, UK, 15-17 April 2007, 815-820.

14. Liu, G. P., S C Chai and **D. Rees,** Networked Predictive Control of Internet/Intranet Based Systems, Proceedings of the 25th Chinese control Conference, Harbin, Heilongjiang, August, 2006.

15. Hu Wenshun, G P Liu **and David Rees,** Design and Implementation of Networked Predictive Control Systems Based on Round Trip Time delay Measurement, *Proceedings of the 2006 American Control Conference, Minneapolis, Minnesota,* USA, 2006, WeA20.5, 674-679.

16. Xia Yuanqing, S. S. Ge, G. P. Liu, P. Shi and **D. Rees,** Robust adaptive sliding Mode control for Uncertain Time Delay systems, *Proceedings of the 2006 American Control Conference, Minneapolis, Minnesota,* USA, 2006, ThC10.3, 3855-3860

17. Liu G. P. **and D. Rees,** Stability Criterion of Networked Predictive Control Systems with Random Network Delay, *Proceedings of the 44th IEEE Conference on Decision and Control, and European Control Conference 2005,* Seville, Dec., 2005, MoA06.5, 203-208

18. Malhotra Khamish, Stephen Gardner, **David Rees,** Evaluating embedded mobile internet for remote patient monitoring applications, *MedNet 2005, 10th World Congress on Internet in Medicine,* Prague, Czech Republic, December 2005.

19. Ouyang Hua, Liu Guoping, **Rees D.,** Robust networked predictive control for systems with random network delay, *Proceedings of the 16th IFAC World Congress,* Prague, July, 2005.

20. Liu Guoping, Xia Y., **Rees D.,** Predictive control of networked systems with random delays, *Proceedings of the 16th IFAC World Congress,* Prague, July, 2005.

21. **Liu Guoping,** Mu J. X., **Rees D.,** Networked predictive control of Systems with random networked transmission delay – a polynomial approach, *Proceedings of the 16th IFAC World Congress,* Prague, July 2005.

22. Xia Yuanqing, Shi Peng, Liu Guoping, **Rees D.,** Stochastic sliding mode control for systems with Markovian jump

parameters, *Proceedings of the 16th IFAC World Congress*, Prague, July, 2005.

23. Chai Senchun, Liu Guoping, **Rees D.**, Design and implementation of networked predictive control systems, *Proceedings of the 16th IFAC World Congress*, Prague, July, 2005.

24. Mu Junxia, G. P. Liu **and David Rees**, Design of robust networked predictive control systems, *Proceedings of the American Control Conference, Portland*, OR, USA, 2005, WeB03.4, 638-643.

25. Malhotra Khamish, S. Gardner, **D. Rees**, Evaluation of GPRS enabled secure remote patient monitoring system, *12th International Conference on Analytical and stochastic modelling techniques and applications* (co-sponsored by IEEE UK, RI Computer Chapter and ECIST COST Action 290), Riga, Latvia, June 2005.

26. Solomou M. and **D. Rees**, Signal quality measures for non-parametric identification of linear systems, *UKACC International Conference on Control, Bath, UK, September, 2004, ID-014*.

27. Liu G. P., J. X. Mu and **D Rees**, Networked predictive control of systems with random communication delay, *UKACC International Conference on Control, Bath, UK, September, 2004, ID-01*.

28. Mu, J.X., **D. Rees**, G.P. Liu, Comparison of approximate and nonlinear model predictive control designs for aircraft gas turbines – A simulation study, *UKACC International Conference on Control*, Bath, 2004, ID –055.

29. Mu J.X., **D. Rees**, G.P. Liu, Design and stability analysis of networked predictive control systems, *UKACC International Conference on Control*, Bath, 2004, ID –003.

30. Mu J. and **D. Rees**, Approximate model predictive control for gas turbines, *Proceedings of the American Control Conference*, Boston, USA, 2004, FrP16., 5704-5709.

31. Mu J. and **D. Rees,** Nonlinear model predictive control for gas turbines, *Proceedings of ASME Turbo Expo Congress, Vienna, Austria, June 2004, GT2004-53146, 1-8.*

32. Solomou Michael, and **David Rees,** System modelling in the presence of nonlinear Distortions, *IEEE Instrumentation and Measurement Conference,* Cernobbio, Italy, May 2004, 1601-1606.

33. Solomou Michael, and **David Rees,** Frequency domain analysis of nonlinear distortions on linear FRF measurements, *IEEE Instrumentation and Measurement Conference,* Cernobbio, Italy, May 2004, .

34. Solomou Michael, **David Rees** and Neophytos Chiras, Controller design for systems suffering nonlinear distortions, *13th IFAC Symposium on System Identification,* Rotterdam, August, 2003, 1201-1206.

35. Solomou Michael, and **David Rees,** Frequency domain analysis of nonlinear distrortion on linear FRF measurements, *IEEE Instrumentation and Measurement Technology Conference,* Vail, USA, May, 2003, 1653-1658.

36. Mu Junxia, **David Rees,** and Neophytos Chiras, Optimum gain-scheduling PID controllers for gas turbine engines based on NARMAX and neural network models, *ASME Turbo Expo Congress,* Atlanta, Geogia, USA, June 2003, GT-2003-38667, 1-8.

37. Chiras N., C. Evans and **D. Rees,** Nonlinear gas turbine modelling using feedforward neural networks, *Proceedings of ASME Turbo Expo Congress,* Amsterdam, Netherlands, 2002, GT-2002-30035, 1-8.

38. Mu J., **D. Rees,** C. Evans and N. Chiras, Design of optimum controllers for gas turbine engine, *Proceedings of the 4th Asian Control Conference,* Singapore, 2002, WM9-24, 826-832.

39. Chiras Neophytos, Ceri Evans, **David Rees** and Michael Solomou, Nonlinear system modelling:How to estimate the

highest significant order, *IEEE Instrumentation and Measurement Technology Conference*, Anchorage, AK, USA, 21-23 May 2002, ISBN 0-7805-7218-2, 353-358.

40. Solomou Michael, Ceri Evans, **David Rees** and Neophytos Chiras, Frequency domain analysis of nonlinear systems driven by multiharmonic signals, *IEEE Instrumentation and Measurement Technology Conference*, Anchorage, AK, USA, 21-23 May 2002-10-28, 799-804.

41. Solomou Michael, Ceri Evans and **David Rees**, Measuring the best linear approximation of systems suffering nonlinear distortions: an alternative method, *IEEE Instrumentation and Measurement Technology Conference*, Anchorage, AK, USA, 21-23 May 2002-10-28, 943-948.

42. Chiras Neophytos, Ceri Evans, and **David Rees**, Recent developments on the modelling of aircraft gas turbines, *The 3rd International conference on control theory and applications*, Pretoria, South Africa, December 12-14, 2001, CD ref: WA03-2.

43. Chiras N, C Evans and **D. Rees**, Global nonlinear modeling of gas turbine dynamics using NARMAX structures, *ASME turbo Expo' 2001 Congress, New Orleans, 2001-GT-19,* 1-8.

44. Evans C., N. Chiras, N. Guillaume and **D. Rees**, Multivariable modelling of gas turbine dynamics, *ASME turbo Expo' 2001 Congress, New Orleans, 2001-GT-0018,* 1-8.

45. Chiras, N., C. Evans and **D. Rees**, Nonlinear modelling and validation of an aircraft gas turbine, *Proceedings of the 5th IFAC Symposium Nonlinear Control Systems,* St. Petersburg, 2001, (CD-ROM).

46. Chiras Neophytos, Ceri Evans, and **David Rees**, Recent developments on the modelling of aircraft gas turbines, *The 3rd International conference on control theory and applications*, Pretoria, South Africa, December 12-14, 2001, CD ref: WA03-2.

47. Solomou M., C. Evans and **D. Rees**, Crest factor minimisation in the frequency domain, *Proceedings of the 18th IEEE Instrumentation and Measurement Technology Conference*, Budapest, Hungary, Vol. 2, ISBN: 0-7803-6646-8, May 21-23, 2001, 1375-1381.

48. Chiras N., C. Evans and **D. Rees**, Linear and nonlinear gas turbine computer modelling, *Proceedings of the UKACC International conference - Control 2000*, Cambridge, September 4-7, 2000, CD ROM - Ref. Session 1A Identification 1.

49. Chiras Neophytos, Ceri Evans, and **David Rees**, Nonlinear gas turbine modelling using NARMAX structures, *Proceedings of the 17th IEEE Instrumentation and Measurement Technology Conference*, Baltimore, Maryland, USA, Vol. 3, ISBN: 0-7803-5890-2, May 1-4, 2000, 1278-1284.

50. Evans Ceri, and **David Rees**, Nonlinear distortions and multisine signals-Part I: Measuring the best linear approximation, *Proceedings of the 16th IEEE Instrumentation and Measurement Technology Conference*, Venice, Italy, Vol. 2, ISBN: 0-7803-5276-9, May 24-26, 1999, 1038-1046.

51. Evans Ceri, and **David Rees**, Nonlinear distortions and multisine signals-Part II: Minimising the distortion, *Proceedings of the 16th IEEE Instrumentation and Measurement Technology Conference*, Venice, Italy, Vol. 2, ISBN: 0-7803-5276-9, May 24-26, 1999, 1047-1053.

52. Borrel Antoni, Ceri Evans and **David Rees**, Identification of aircraft gas turbine dynamics using frequency-domain techniques, *Proceedings of the UKACC International conference - Control '98*, Swansea, Conference Publication No. 455, Vol. 2, Sep. 1-4, 1998, 1372-1378.

53. Evans Ceri, Antoni Borrell and **David Rees**, Validation of thermodynamic gas turbine models using frequency-domain techniques, *Proceedings of the IEEE Instrumentation and*

Measurement Technology Conference, St Paul, Minnesota, USA, Vol. 2, ISBN: 0-7803-4798-6, May 18-21, 1998, 993-998.

54. Evans Ceri, and **David Rees**, Experiment design for gas turbine modelling, *Proceedings of the IEEE Instrumentation and Measurement Technology Conference*, Ottawa, Canada, Vol. 1, ISBN: 0-7803-3748-4, May 19-21, 1997, 558-A-558-G.

55. Evans Ceri, Michael Weiss, Teresa Escobet, Joseba Quevedo, **David Rees** and Lee Jones, Borrel Antoni, Ceri Evans and **David Rees**, Identification in the time and frequency domains: a comparison using the EEC bench-mark model, *Proceedings of the UKACC International conference – Control '96, Exeter*, Conference Publication No. 427, Vol. 2, Sept. 2-5, 1996, 1290-1296.

56. Weiss M., C. Evans, **D. Rees,** L. Jones, Structure Identification of block-orientated nonlinear systems using periodic test signals, *Proceedings of the IEEE Instrumentation and Measurement Technology Conference*, Brussels, Belgium, Vol. 1, ISBN: 0-7803-3313-6, June 4-6, 1996, 8-13.

57. **Rees D.**, M. Weiss, C. Evans and L. Jones, A measurement and system identification setup controlled through a graphical user interface, *Proceedings of 8ᵗʰ IFAC symposium on Information control problems in manufacturing*, Beijing, October, 1995.

58. M. Weiss, **D. Rees**, C. Evans and L. Jones, A measurement and system identification setup to estimate a model for control purposes, *Proceedings of IChemE Conference on Advanced Process Control 4*, York, 1995, September 27-28, 85-92.

59. Evans Ceri, **David Rees**, Lee Jones, and Michael Weiss, Periodic signals for measuring nonlinear Volterra kernels, *Proceedings of the IEEE Instrumentation and Measurement Technology Conference*, Waltham, Massachusetts, USA, ISBN: 0-7803-2616-4, April 24-26, 1995, 10-15.

60. Evans, C., **D.Rees**, L Jones and D. Hill, Measuring and identification of gas turbine dynamics in the presence of noise and nonlinearities, *Proceedings of the IEEE Instrumentation and Measurement Technology Conference*, Hamamatsu, Japan, Vol. 2. ISBN: 0-7803-1881-1, May 10-12, 1994, 609-614.

61. Evans C., **David Rees**, Lee Jones and Dave Hill, Time and frequency domain identification of jet engine dynamics: problems and solutions, *10ᵗʰ IFAC Symposium on System Identification*, Copenhagen, Denmark, Vol. 2, ISBN 87-7748-034-1, Publication No. 389, July 4-6, 1994, 243-248.

62. Evans D. C., **D. Rees**, and D. L. Jones, Identifying linear models of systems suffering nonlinear distortions, *Proceedings IEE Control '94 conference*, Warwick, March 21-24, 1994, 288-296.

63. Watson V. E., **D. Rees**, G. White, Evaluation of creep effects on jointed and unjointed non-metallic strength members in optical communication cables, *Proceedings of the Forty-second International Wire and Cable Symposium*, St Louis, Missouri, USA, Nov. 15-18, 1993, 56-64.

64. Evans Ceri, **David Rees**, and Lee Jones, Nonlinear disturbance errors in system identification using multisine test signals, *Proceedings of the IEEE Instrumentation and Measurement Technology Conference*, Irvine, California, USA, ISBN: 0-7803-1230-9, May 18-20, 1993, 258-263.

65. Luk C. K., M. G. Jayne, **D. Rees**, The development of an integrated induction motor drive system using a network of transputers, *IEE Colloquium on developments in real-time control for induction motor drives*, London, Digest No. 1993/024, 1993.

66. Wiess M., **D. Rees**, and J. Silvestre, Knowledge-based self-tuning controllers, *Proceedings of the 28ᵗʰ University Power Engineers Conference*, Staffordshire University, 1993.

67. **Rees D.,** D. L. Jones and D. C. Evans, Design of low peak factor multisine test signals for parametric and non-parametric system identification, *Proceedings of the Canadian Conference and Exhibition (ISA) on Industrial Automation,* Montreal, ISBN: 2-9802946-0-8, June 1-3, 1992, 19.5-19.10.

68. **Rees D.,** D. L. Jones and D. C. Evans, Practical considerations in the design of multisine test signals for system identification, *Proceedings of the IEEE Instrumentation and Measurement Technology Conference,* New York, USA, ISBN: 0-7803-0641-4, May 12-14, 1992, 174-179.

69. Luk, C. K. P., M. G. Jayne, **D. Rees,** D. W. Schaper, A digital model for a three-phase induction motor drive using a personal computer software package, Proceedings of the *Fifth IFAC/IMACS Symposium on Computer aided Design in Control Systems,* Swansea, UK, July 1992. 589-594.

70. Morland G., **D. Rees,** G. White, An evaluation of the inter-relationships between rheological data of filling compounds and fibre optic performance, *Proceedings of the Fortieth International Wire and Cable Symposium,* St Louis, Missouri, USA, Nov. 18-21, 1991, 469-475.

71. Luk, C. K. P., M. G. Jayne, **D. Rees,** The transputer control of variable speed induction motor drives, Proceedings of the *Fourth European Conference on Power Electronics,* Florence, Vol. 1, September 3-6, 1991, 574-579.

72. **Rees D.,** and D. L. Jones, Design and application of non-binary low peak factor signals for system dynamic measurement, *Proceedings IEE Control '91 conference,* Edinburgh, Vol. 1, March 25-28, 1991 644-650.

73. Wilkinson B., and **D. Rees,** Performance evaluation of a pattern recognition adaptive controller, *Proceedings of the 1990 European Simulation Symposium on Intelligent Process Control Design and Scheduling,* Ghent, Belgium, ISBN 0-911801-83-9, Nov., 1990, 85-90.

74. Sutton P. A., J. L. L. Roberts, A. T. Summers, A. Phoenix, **D. Rees**, Development of a non-destructive test for microbend loss mechanisms, *Proceedings of the 2nd Bangor Communication Symposium,* University of Wales, Bangor, May 1990.

75. **Rees D.**, Design of non-binary signals with low peak factors, *IEE Colloquium Digest on Multifrequency testing for system identification,* London, Digest No: 1990/097, June 8, 1990, 4/1-4/6.

76. Jones D. L. and **D. Rees,** Aliasing problems associated with the implementation of multifrequency test strategies, *IEE Colloquium Digest on Multifrequency testing for system identification,* London, Digest No: 1990/097, June 8, 1990, 5/1-5/4.

77. Sutton P. A., J. L. L. Roberts, A. T. Summers, A. Phoenix, **D. Rees**, Development of a non-destructive test for microbend loss mechanisms in cabled fibre, *Proceedings of the Thirty-eighth International Wire and Cable Symposium,* Atlanta, Georgia, USA, Nov., 14-16, 1989, 450-455.

78. Roberts J. L. L., **D. Rees** and H. Jones, Optical fibre cable design using an expert system, *Proceedings of Bejing International Conference on system simulation and scientific computing,* Beijing, Vol. 1., ISBN 0-08-037881-1, October 23-26, 1989, 467-470.

79. Luk, C. K. P., M. G. Jayne, **D. Rees,** Use of transputer for pulse-width modulated (PWM) inverters, *Proceedings of the 24th University Power Engineers Conference,* 1989, 81-84.

80. Mohan Manoj, David Diani and **David Rees**, Development of a flight standard power conditioning and control system for the T5 ion thruster, *Proceedings of the 20th International Electric Propulsion Conference (AIAA/DGLR/JSASS),* Garmisch-Partenkirchen, Germany, ISBN 3-922010-40-7, October 3-6, 1988, 283-291.

81. Jones D. L., and **D. Rees,** Architecture of an intelligent, novel, high performance frequency response analyser,

Proceedings of ISMM, mini and microcomputers and their applications (MIMI 88), Sant Feliu, Spain, 1988, 470-473.

82. **Rees D.,** Application of digital signal processors to controller implementations, *Proceedings of IMACS 1988, the 12th world congress on scientific computing,* Paris, France, ISBN 2-9502908-0-9, Vol. 3, 1988, 268-271.

83. Roberts J. L. L., **D. Rees,** and H. Jones, Development of an expert system for fibre optic cable design, *Proceedings of the 8th International workshop on Expert Systems and their applications,* Avignon, May 30-June 3, 1988.

84. Jones D. L., **D. Rees,** A frequency response analyser based on composite frequency test signals, *Proceedings of ASME conference on Modelling and Simulation,* Karlsruhe, Germany, July, 1987, 1-12.

85. Jones D. L., **D. Rees,** System testing using low-peak factor composite signals, *Proceedings of ASME conference on Modelling and Simulation,* Cairo, March, 1987, 1-4.

86. **Rees D.,** Controller implementation using digital signal processors, *IEE Colloquium on Novel architectures and algorithms for controllers,* London, Digest No: 1987/18, February 2, 1987, 2/1-2/4.

87. **Rees, D.,** System identification using composite frequency signals with low peak factors, *Proceedings of International AMSE Conference on Modelling and Simulation,* Sorrento, Vol. 1&2, 1986, 644-650.

88. **Rees D.,** Controller implementation using a monolithic signal processor, *Proceedings of ISMM, mini and microcomputers and their applications (MIMI 85),* Sant Feliu, Spain, ISBN 7488-121-8, June 25-28, 1985, 417-420.

89. Gardner S. and **D. Rees,** Simulation of the telephone wire insulation process in cable manufacturing using I.S.I.S., *Proceedings of the 1984 UKSC conference on computer simulation,* Bath, ISBN 0-408-01504-7, Sept. 12-14, 1984, 289-301.

90. **Rees D.**, and P. A. Witting, Use of novel processor architectures for controller realization, *Proceedings of the IEEE/ EUREL 6ᵗʰ European Conference on Electrotechnics – computers in communication and control*, Brighton, PPL Conference Publication No. 22, ISBN 0-86341-029-4, Sep. 26-28, 1984, 108-113.

91. Gardner S., and **D. Rees**, Recent developments in the modelling and simulation of the process of insulating telephone wire with foamed polyethylene, *Proceedings of IASTED Conference on Applied Modelling and Simulation*, Nice, France, ISBN 0-88986-063-7, June 19-21, 1984, 159-162.

92. **Rees D.** and M. White, The control of an unstable open-loop system by means of discrete algorithms using a microcomputer, *Proceedings of the IERE Conference on real time control of electromechanical systems*, London, IERE Conference Publication No. 58, ISBN 0-903748-53-6, March 6-7, 1984, 13-19.

93. **Rees D.**, F.F.R.I.P. – A program for system identification using the discrete Fourier transform, *Proceedings of the 1981 UKSC conference on computer simulation*, Harrogate, ISBN 0-86103-051-6, May 13-15, 1981, 236-244.

94. **Rees D.** and A. Pennington, A microprocessor controlled digital frequency response analyser, *Proceedings of the IERE Conference on microprocessors in automation and communications*, London, IERE Conference Publication No. 48, ISBN 0-903748-43-6, Jan. 27-29, 1981, 243-252.

95. Pennington A. and **D. Rees**, Automated frequency response testing using a microprocessor, *The 3rd British conference and teaching the use of microprocessors,*, Leeds Polytechnic, 1980, 1-9.

96. **Rees D.**, System identification in the presence of non linearities using deterministic signals and the fast Fourier transform, *IEE Colloquium Digest on Identification of Nonlinear*

Systems, London, Digest No: 1978/31, May 16, 1978, 4/1-4/6.

97. **Rees D.** System identification using spectral methods, *The 2nd British conference on teaching of correlation and spectral techniques in Higher education*, Leeds Polytechnic, 1978, 1-13.

98. Doyle D. and **D. Rees**, Experience in the use of a microprocessor based instrument for rapid frequency response measurement, *Conference and teaching the usage of microprocessors*, Leeds Polytechnic, 1978, 1-10.

99. **Rees D.**, Automatic testing of dynamic systems using multi-frequency signals and the discrete Fourier transform, *Proceedings of the IEE Conference on new developments in automatic testing*, Brighton, IEE Conference Publication No. 158, ISBN 0-85296184-7, November 30- December 2, 1977, 24-27.

100.**Rees D.** and D. Doyle, A microprocessor based instrument for rapid frequency response measurement, *Proceedings of the IERE Conference on programmable instruments*, Teddington, IERE Conference Publication No. 38, ISBN 0-903748-33-9, November 22-24, 1977, 61-71.

101.Lamb, J. D. and **D. Rees**, Digital processing of system responses to pseudo-random binary sequences to obtain frequency response characteristics using the fast Fourier transform, *Proceedings of the IEE Conference on the use of digital computers in measurement*, York, Conference Publication No. 103, ISBN 0-85296114-6, Sept. 24-27, 1973. 141-146.

V

OVERSEAS TRAVEL

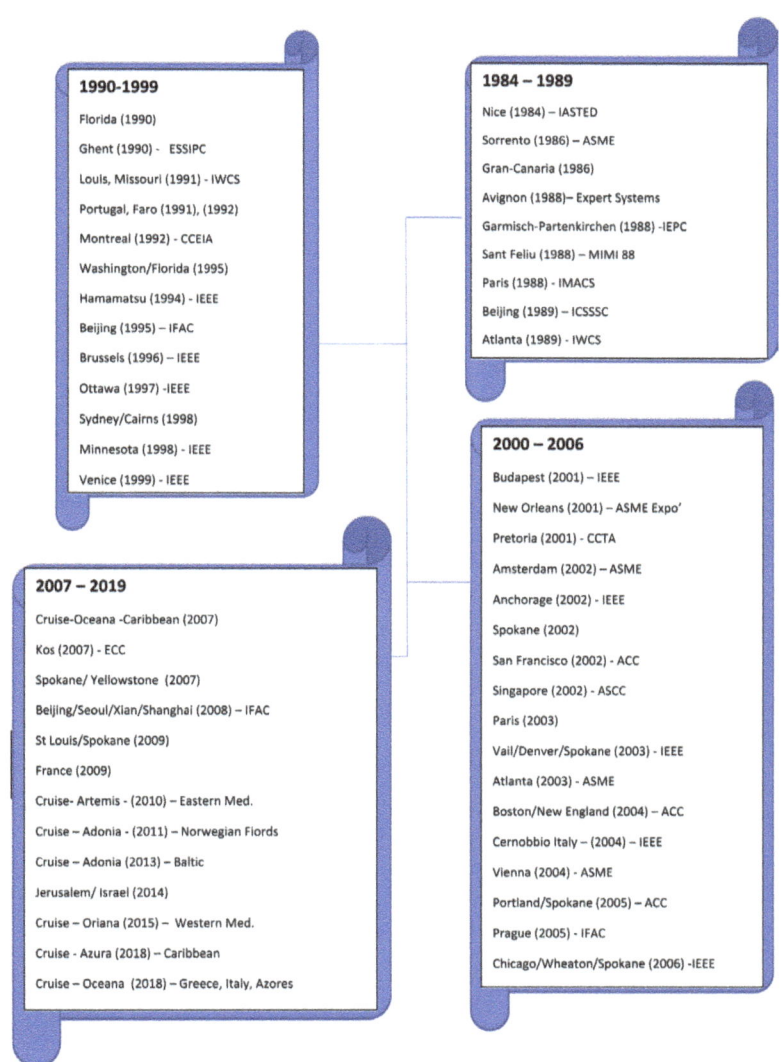

1990-1999

Florida (1990)

Ghent (1990) - ESSIPC

Louis, Missouri (1991) - IWCS

Portugal, Faro (1991), (1992)

Montreal (1992) - CCEIA

Washington/Florida (1995)

Hamamatsu (1994) - IEEE

Beijing (1995) – IFAC

Brussels (1996) – IEEE

Ottawa (1997) -IEEE

Sydney/Cairns (1998)

Minnesota (1998) - IEEE

Venice (1999) - IEEE

1984 – 1989

Nice (1984) – IASTED

Sorrento (1986) – ASME

Gran-Canaria (1986)

Avignon (1988)– Expert Systems

Garmisch-Partenkirchen (1988) -IEPC

Sant Feliu (1988) – MIMI 88

Paris (1988) - IMACS

Beijing (1989) – ICSSSC

Atlanta (1989) - IWCS

2000 – 2006

Budapest (2001) – IEEE

New Orleans (2001) – ASME Expo'

Pretoria (2001) - CCTA

Amsterdam (2002) – ASME

Anchorage (2002) - IEEE

Spokane (2002)

San Francisco (2002) - ACC

Singapore (2002) - ASCC

Paris (2003)

Vail/Denver/Spokane (2003) - IEEE

Atlanta (2003) - ASME

Boston/New England (2004) – ACC

Cernobbio Italy – (2004) – IEEE

Vienna (2004) - ASME

Portland/Spokane (2005) – ACC

Prague (2005) - IFAC

Chicago/Wheaton/Spokane (2006) -IEEE

2007 – 2019

Cruise-Oceana -Caribbean (2007)

Kos (2007) - ECC

Spokane/ Yellowstone (2007)

Beijing/Seoul/Xian/Shanghai (2008) – IFAC

St Louis/Spokane (2009)

France (2009)

Cruise- Artemis - (2010) – Eastern Med.

Cruise – Adonia - (2011) – Norwegian Fiords

Cruise – Adonia (2013) – Baltic

Jerusalem/ Israel (2014)

Cruise – Oriana (2015) – Western Med.

Cruise - Azura (2018) – Caribbean

Cruise – Oceana (2018) – Greece, Italy, Azores

VI

REFERENCES

1. The History of Penygroes and District. 1815 to 1915; John Davies, Penygroes Eisteddfod, May 12th 1917. [Published in Penygroes, Caerbryn a Blaenau' History of the area in pictures', 2011]

2. WIKIPEDIA, Entry on Penygroes, Carmarthenshire, 2020

3. *Contemporary Welsh Preachers Volume 1 'Where is faith? Author Llewelyn Jenkins, Aberystwyth'. P78,* Leaping Cat Press, 2004.

4. 'The Welsh Revival of 1904', Eifion Evans, Bryntirion Press, 2000, ISBN 1 850490376

5. 'The use of Hybrid Computing in the Analysis of Steel Rolling'; J. W. Golten and David Rees. IEEE Transactions on Electronic Computers, Volume EC-16, Number 6, December, 1967. pp. 717-722

6. David Martyn Lloyd Jones, Vol. 1 &2, Iain H. Murray, The Banner of Truth Trust, 1982 & 1990, ISBN 0 85151 353 0; 085151 564 9.

7. 'To know and Serve God' A biography of James I. Packer, Alister McGrath, Hodder & Stoughton, 1997, ISBN 0 340 56571 3.

8. 'Evangelism and the Sovereignty of God', J I Packer, IVP, ISBN 9781844744985

9. 'The Death of Death in the Death of Christ', John Owen, The Banner of Truth Trust, ISBN 0 85151 382 4

10. 'Llanarthney Past and Present', Tom & Delyth Jones, Published by Carmarthenshire County Council, 2002, ISBN 0 906821 59 2P

11. 'Bread of Heaven' The life and work of William Williams, Pantycelyn, Eifion Evans, 2010, ISBN 978 1 85049 24 05

12. 'Robert Ferrar – Yorkshire Monk, Reformation Bishop, and Martyr in Wales', Andrew J. Brown, 1997, ISBN 0 9528271 1 5

13. 'William Tyndale on Priests and Preachers' Andrew J. Brown, 1996, ISBN 0 9528271 0 7

14. 'Developments in automating the design of fibre-optic cable', Llyr Roberts, MPhil thesis, Nov. 1988.

15. 'A history of the Brethren Movement', F. Roy Coad, The Paternoster Press, 1968, SBN: 85364 085 8

16. 'The Origins of the Brethren', Harold H. Rowden, Pickering & Inglis Ltd, 1967, SBN 7208 0000 5

17. 'Gathering to his Name', Tim Grass, Paternoster Press, 2006, ISBN 1-84227-220-9

18. *When God's Voice is Heard*: Essays on preaching presented to Dick Lucas, Green and Jackman (1995). (Leicester: IVP) ISBN 0-85110-656-0

19. 'The Chappo Collection', David Mansfield, Grace Abounding Books, 2017, ISBN 978-0-6481637-0-

20. 'Identification of Linear and Nonlinear Systems using Multisine Signals with a Gas Turbine Application. Ceri Evans,1998, PhD Thesis, University of Glamorgan.

21. Dawkins 1995, 'River out of Eden, A Darwinian view of life' ISBN 9781857994056.

About the Author

David Rees is a father and grandfather, who is proud of his Welsh roots and appreciative of the influences that have shaped him to make him the person that he now is. He has spent over 50 years pursuing a career in Electrical and Electronic Engineering, initially in industry and laterally as University lecturer and researcher. The dominant influence in his life has been a Christian  world view, which has shaped his priorities and activities, including a lifetime commitment to Church life and mission.

Lightning Source UK Ltd.
Milton Keynes UK
UKHW020220101120
373087UK00004B/274/J